P9-CEJ-921

WILD COMMUNION

WILD COMMUNION

Experiencing Peace in Nature

Ruth Baetz

■ HAZELDEN®

Hazelden
Center City, Minnesota 55012-0176
1-800-328-0094
1-612-257-1331 (FAX)
http://www.hazelden.org

© 1997 by Ruth Baetz
All rights reserved. Published 1997
Printed in the United States of America
No portion of this publication may be reproduced
in any manner without the written
permission of the publisher.

Library of Congress Cataloging-in-Publication Data
Baetz, Ruth.
    Wild communion: experiencing peace in nature/Ruth
    Baetz.
      p. cm.
    Includes bibliographical references.
    ISBN 1-56838-187-5
    1. Nature—Psychological aspects. 2. Meditation. I.Title.
  BF353.5.N37B 1997
  155.9′ 1—dc21   97-27080
                                                              CIP

EDITOR'S NOTE
Hazelden offers a variety of information on chemical dependency and related areas. Our publications do not necessarily
represent Hazelden's programs, nor do they officially speak
for any Twelve Step organization.

The author, in association with Treemendous Seattle, will
facilitate the planting of two trees for every one tree used in
the manufacture of this book.

This book is dedicated to Rachel Carson—

your courage and passion for nature has touched us all.

Apparently I have never made it clear that I consider my contributions to scientific fact far less important than my attempts to awaken an emotional response to the world of nature.

—Rachel Carson

Contents

Acknowledgments

First I would like to thank my parents. Although we lived in a big city, they managed to foster in me a love of nature. Dad took us to natural beauty spots on his short vacations, and Mom always pointed out the miniature wonders along the trail.

I would also like to thank my larger family: all the members of The Nature Conservancy, the Sierra Club, the National Audubon Society, the Mountaineers, and every other group, large and small, that works to preserve the natural world and instill in people a respect for nature. You sustain the web that makes this book possible. In this family, I include all the native cultures that have preserved the integrity of the earth's ecology and all the conservationists that have gone before us.

My agent Kay Kidde offered invaluable suggestions and her "Brava!" after every revision kept up my spirits. I appreciate her dedication and her unwavering belief in the book. Her colleague Laura Langlie was always an encouraging and knowledgeable resource.

Nancy Manahan and my mother-in-law Impy Weir not only edited sections of the book, they nearly loved this book into existence.

Thanks to my enthusiastic team at Hazelden for enhancing the clarity and beauty of the book, especially my editor, Kate Kjorlien.

Thanks to the Penfields and the Foxes—Jim, Georgia, Kedzie, Jane, and Kate—for sharing Beachwood with me.

Thanks to Susan Johnson, Linda Damico, Sherrod Mohr and Tina Bammes for early feedback. Thanks to Mondi Mallory and Connie Wolfe for being on my spiritual support team. Thanks to Kate Thayer, Joan Allen, Taen Scherer, and Barbara Morgan for being consistent cheerleaders.

And last, but not at all least, thanks to my partner Sandra Jo who not only took every step with me, but often carried the gear as well.

WILD COMMUNION

*Climb the mountains and get their good tidings.
Nature's peace will flow into you as sunshine
flows into trees. The winds will blow their own
freshness into you, and the storms their energy,
while cares will drop off like autumn leaves.*

—John Muir

INTRODUCTION

When I turned thirty-three, I decided to do something different. I decided to go alone to the Canadian Rocky Mountains.

I had been a city slicker all my life. I had grown up in Chicago, where the great outdoors was a baseball diamond and "playing jungle" meant slinking among the trash cans in the alley. As an adult, I was a social worker in a housing project and a therapist in private practice. Any spare time went to community meetings or political events. I didn't have much time for the "good tidings" of mountains.

But for my thirty-third birthday I wanted an adventure, and taking my first solo car-camping trip definitely qualified. I packed enough food and books to last three months, even though my trip was only going to last three weeks. I

1

worried about bears and flat tires and slippery cliffs. By the time I actually left home, I thought I was ready for anything. I was wrong. I hadn't prepared for bliss.

Bliss was not a feeling I had ever experienced before. I had felt happy or delighted or exhilarated. But this was a different order of emotion. This was off my internal Richter scale.

In the Canadian Rockies, joy and life-shaking realizations erupted within me daily. I was constantly awed by magnificence. All I had to do was get myself to a private spot by a wildflower meadow or a glacial pond, and some unnamed vibrant energy would wash through me.

As the end of my three weeks drew near, I started to get depressed. How could I go back to my city life? How could I leave ecstasy? I felt like the patriarch in *The Source* who stays in the desert for six years after he is ordered to leave it because he is afraid he will lose touch with his deity, El-Shaddai:

> *"El-Shaddai!" the patriarch cried in anguish. . . .*
> *"In the town will we know you as we have known you in the desert?"*
>
> *"Inside the walls it will not be easy for me to speak with you," the deity answered, "but I shall be there."*

I promised myself I would figure out how to have a deep relationship with nature close to home. Surely there was a way to feel the ecstasy and still live in a city.

Needless to say, my promise was easier to make than to keep. In my ordinary life, I had to face all the barriers that kept me out of contact with nature: my work schedule and my guilt at spending "non-productive" time outdoors, for instance. Even when I managed to get myself to a park or a trail, the quiet natural wonders rarely could penetrate my racing mind in the little time I could spare. I felt frustrated and disappointed more often than ecstatic.

I realized I would have to be more purposeful during my visits to nature. I couldn't just sit there and hope I'd be swooped away as I had been in the Rockies. I needed to develop ways to drop my preoccupations and to connect with nature quickly when I was in a local park with limited time; I needed to create methods to deepen my connection when I was in a national park for the weekend so I could bring those more profound experiences home with me as touchstones.

I started to experiment. As a therapist, I drew from the psychotherapy, hypnotherapy, and deep relaxation techniques I used in my practice. As a student of meditation and spirituality, I drew from meditation techniques. As a person with disabilities, I used the skill that comes with having limitations: simplification. Everything had to be as simple and fast as possible because sometimes I couldn't walk far or sit long. To all that, I added a strong dose of perseverance and a willingness to be unorthodox.

3

I communed and I wrote in my journal. I discovered that journal writing is an integral part of the process: When I write while I commune, the process of writing itself helps me stay focused on the experience I'm having. When I write during or immediately afterward, I can record details of my internal reactions I would otherwise forget. And, of course, my written record has allowed me to analyze and tease out the most helpful techniques. The result of my fourteen years of experiments is in your hands: *Wild Communion: Experiencing Peace in Nature.*

Over the years I have come to see communing with nature as more than a way to get a hit of bliss. Sometimes it gives me a deep serenity or a gentle feeling of connectedness. Sometimes it gives me lessons I desperately need, whether the lessons themselves comfort or pain me. Other times communing is the catalyst for a boundary-shattering mystical oneness with the universe that is as frightening as it is ecstatic.

You may commune as part of your spiritual practice or to "get your head together." You may simply do it to reduce your stress and increase your health. An article in *McCall's* magazine reports on the benefits of communing:

> *The need to commune with nature is so ingrained in us, say some psychologists, that contact with the great outdoors is as essential to our well-being as close, personal relationships with others are. . . . "The natural environment has*

> *turned out to be the most powerful setting to reduce mental fatigue we've found," says Kaplan [a psychologist at the University of Michigan]. . . . When your mind is weary and wandering, merely gazing outside at a cluster of trees has been found to be more mentally stimulating than drinking a cup of coffee or eating a candy bar."*

The editors of *The Biophilia Hypothesis* contend that we may need a significant relationship with nature for our mental and physical health because we have evolved amidst a complex web of nature, and the development of our nervous system depends on relating to that web. In an article entitled, "Can one love a plastic tree?" H. Iltis writes, ". . . one of these days we shall find the intricate neurological bases of why a leaf or a lovely flower affects us so very differently than a broken beer bottle."

Perhaps communing is a way to bring a spiritual and emotional—even a mystical—component not just to our personal lives, but to the modern ecological movement as well. It gives us an intimate relationship with nature that can inform our reasoned actions. As the radical philosopher Alan Watts wrote, "If science is actually to become our way of liberation, its theoretical view must be translated into feeling." And in his book, *Earth in the Balance,* Al Gore offers many ways we can each make a difference in the global environmental crisis. He writes, "Perhaps most important, we each need to assess our own relationship to the natural world and renew, at the deepest level of personal integrity, a connection to it."

Wild Communion is both a how-to book and a spiritual adventure book. Each chapter contains easy communing techniques that you can use immediately, and entries from my journals that let you experience vicariously what each technique can do. None of the exercises requires equipment or practice. At the end of each chapter, a quick-reference box summarizes that chapter's techniques so you can refresh your memory easily.

Take this book with you when you go to a wilderness trail or to your local park. Whether you hike for a day or sit in your wheelchair for half an hour, you will get powerful results.

Read this book in your living room before you start your busy day, so you can bring the peace of nature into your ordinary life. Or read it before bedtime. A friend of mine keeps *Wild Communion* on her bedside table and reads a page or two before she goes to sleep. She says the entries give her nice dreams.

While it's easiest to commune when you're alone, you can certainly do it with other people around, too. I've taught most of these techniques to friends. You'll read some of their reactions in the journal entries. Sharing with a friend is a great way to learn and to deepen a friendship.

Feel free to change any of the exercises and any of my terminology to suit your own style. Some of the things I do

will seem unusual to you; let my willingness to be outrageous inspire you to be unconventional too. This is a
chance to give your creativity free rein.

For instance, when I was in the Canadian Rockies, I
named the energy I felt pouring through everything "the
life force." Sometimes I talk to or about the life force when
I commune. If that term seems strange, change it to something you're more comfortable with.

Don't be surprised if you can't zip through this book.
Each journal entry will take you inside an experience that
triggers emotional and sensual reactions. You will learn
better and enjoy yourself more if you slow down and let
your body feel what I'm describing. Maybe you won't finish a chapter each day, but you will have body memories to
draw on when you're out in nature and want to remember
how to commune.

So relax into the chapters. Let them support and
brighten your daily life. Let them help you build a deep,
lasting love affair with the earth.

> I wish I could walk out of that school and find
> myself a place where there are no whites, no black
> folk, no people of any kind! I mean, a place where
> I'd be able to sit still, and get my head together; a
> place where I could walk and walk, and I'd be
> walking on grass, not cement, with glass and
> garbage around. . . . At night, sometimes, when I
> get to feeling real low, I'll climb up the stairs to

our roof, and I'll look at the sky, and I'll say hello
there, you moon and all your babies—stars! I'm
being silly, I know, but up there, I feel I can stop
and think about what's happening to me—it's
the only place I can, the only place.

—twelve-year-old African American girl in a
Boston ghetto who was being bussed to a previously all-
white school (quoted in *The Geography of Childhood*)

In this chapter, you will learn some practical tips that will make communing with nature easier wherever you are.

I
COMMUNING WITH NATURE

What's the difference between looking at a tree and communing with a tree? The philosopher Martin Buber could have been answering that very question when he wrote:

> I contemplate a tree.
>
> I can accept it as a picture. . . . I can feel it as movement. . . . I can assign it to a species. . . . I can dissolve it into a number. . . .
>
> But it can also happen, if will and grace are joined, that as I contemplate the tree I am drawn into a relation, and the tree ceases to be an It. . . .

When I commune with a tree, I am drawn into a relationship with that tree. Buber would say I move from an "I-It" relationship to an "I-Thou" relationship in which the tree and I are equals.

When I commune, I "witness the intelligence within every living thing," as Deepak Chopra says. I feel respect and tenderness and sacredness. Something flows between me and the tree. I feel at home.

Communing touches all aspects of a person. It engages the mind, the emotions, the body, and the spirit.

I developed the communing techniques in *Wild Communion* because I found it difficult to enter this I-Thou relationship with nature when I was outside of wilderness areas. Yet, if anything, I needed the nourishment of communing even more when I was in my everyday life.

If you're like most people, you, too, have limited time to spend in the wilderness. If you want a daily—or even a weekly—relationship with nature, most of that relationship will happen close to home. Unfortunately, modern life is not set up to make communing easy.

Natural areas are often small or next to noisy highways or full of boisterous children. If your community hasn't planned well, natural areas may also be quite a drive from your home.

Schedules today are far too busy to allow time for communing. Like any spiritual practice or exercise routine, time for communing has to be stolen from time spent on the To-Do lists. The latest leisure attractions beckon or demand time much more forcefully than communing ever can. Communing has no publicity department.

Spiritual or contemplative practices are not part of the common dialogue in today's world. Friends ask what movies you've seen, not where you've communed with nature lately.

Modern jobs and chores require speed, efficiency, and logical thinking. The question is always, "How much can you get done?" not, "How peaceful and connected to nature can you feel?"

And so, communing is always an act of individuality, discipline, and personal passion. The urge comes from within, the time is created by determination, and convenient locations are discovered by focused exploration.

Before I describe specific communing exercises, let me give you some tips on the practical aspects of communing. When I began communing in my everyday life, I had to learn the best times (and sometimes even write them into my day planner); find the best places; make sure I felt safe; and figure out what I needed to take with me to be comfortable.

When to Commune

The quality of your communing experience will often be determined by *when* you commune. The playground that is exploding with children at midday may be empty at dawn or dusk. The pasture that is ugly at noon may be stunning at sunrise or moonrise. Your unkempt yard may be magic at midnight.

The time from dusk to dawn generally has more natural

sounds, more silence, and a slower pace. It has fewer people and more privacy. As the evening sky deepens, you can grin unselfconsciously at the beauty of a tree blowing in the wind and no one will see you or interrupt you.

Midweek is also a good time to find privacy in local parks. People with nontraditional work schedules have an advantage here. I've arranged my schedule so I can work on Sundays and evenings. Not only does that give my working clients convenient appointment times, it also gives me midweek time to commune when most people are at work. School bus drivers and stay-at-home moms may find peaceful middays; waiters, nurses, and police officers often have schedules that allow them free time during the week. Some people negotiate to work four ten-hour days so they can have a day off in the middle of the week. Take advantage of any flexibility in your schedule to look for those windows of opportunity when local natural areas may be quieter and less populated.

You will often find more privacy and stunning beauty during challenging weather. The arboretum is empty during dramatic windstorms and the vacant lot down the block is unpopulated during the symphonic sounds of a rain. With warm clothes or a raincoat and rain pants, you can be perfectly comfortable communing while your neighbors are locked indoors. Porches and picnic shelters allow you to soak up the sounds and smells when it's pouring too hard for just a raincoat. Communing after a rainstorm, when the grass is still wet and the trees are still dripping, will surround you with a gourmet's buffet of delectable smells but few other humans. Fog shrouding a popular viewpoint also offers privacy and gentle magic.

Go off-season. Off-season doesn't just mean deep winter. The emptiest days at Seattle's Washington Park Arboretum are in midsummer. The park is dripping with people when the spring flowers are in bloom or the autumn colors are brilliant, but it's just green in the summer, and most people are off camping or sight-seeing.

The other important *when* factor is your body. After fourteen years of communing, I still can't commune well when I'm too tired, too hungry, too hot or cold, or too uncomfortable. A yogi may be able to meditate on a bed of nails after days of fasting, but I can't. So I recommend attending to the needs of your body before you begin.

Where to Commune

Finding spots to commune takes some time, some creativity, and a sense of adventure. You are most likely to commune regularly if you can go to natural places that are only five to ten minutes away, so start your search close to your regular routes of travel. What parks or natural nooks are near your home, your workplace, your grocery store, your best friend's house, your bookstore?

In the beginning, searching out these places will take

perseverance, and you will have your share of failures. That private-looking ravine is really a mosquito-infested swamp, and more traffic runs past this tree than you can tolerate, for instance. But after a certain amount of trial and error, you will have your own personal list of favorite places to commune.

Don't despair if you don't live near many official parks. Lobby for more parks and green belts, of course, but until those new parks are created, look for the unusual communing places.

You can commune with clouds or the open sky from balconies, roofs, and the platforms of jungle gyms in playgrounds. Sometimes dead ends have a bit of land at the end of them or stairs that continue down steep hillsides. Either one may offer treetop views or privacy. Cemeteries and churchyards can be quiet and beautiful.

The unplowed edges of crop fields or the windbreaks between fields can be a haven for wildlife and for you. The hedgerows separating pastures in England are now such important wildlife refuges that the British Parliament is considering a law that would require farmers to get special permission to remove a hedgerow. Many farmers in the United States have put a portion of their land into a land trust or wildlife preserve program. Someone who owns land near you may give you permission to commune in exchange for some help with maintenance.

If you want to block noise, look for spots that already

have natural sounds: a gurgling creek, a lapping lake, or trees that rustle in the wind. A small hill between you and traffic can create an island of quiet. When all else fails, use foam earplugs. While they block out the lovely natural sounds, earplugs are very handy when the jarring mechanical sounds of lawn mowers and chain saws are just too much.

You will find your own special-situation spots. You may find a thick-limbed tree that can protect you from light rains, a breezy ravine that will cool you during midday heat, or a boulder that can shelter you from the prevailing winds. You may learn that a particular sprinkler in summer attracts a circus of birds, and that a certain tree-lined hilltop puts on the best show in a high wind. All these discoveries will give you a larger sense of home.

Blocking out the distractions of people can be a challenge. Try focusing away from them. If you commune facing the trunk of a tree or looking up into its branches, humans will be out of sight, at least. If you walk into the bushes between the paths full of joggers, or paddle twenty feet away from the crowded lakeshore on an air mattress, you may discover surprising peace and privacy. Anywhere you are, you can close your eyes. You may find, in fact, that closing your eyes opens you to a new favorite activity: communing through your senses of smell, hearing and feeling. There are more tips for blocking out distractions in chapter 3 "Settling In," in chapter 6 "Using Mantras," and in chapter 7 "Getting Close."

If you can learn to commune with the air, you can commune almost anywhere. You can open your living-room window and commune with the play of the breeze across your face. You can lie in bed beside your open window and commune with the ever-changing perfumes of spring. I've even communed in the seventh-floor office of a dentist, enjoying gusts blowing in the window at that elevation.

While communing close to home will allow you to have a nourishing consistent relationship with nature, it's also important to go to natural areas farther away from the pull of your everyday life. As I mentioned earlier, I first learned communing in wild nature and then transferred my learnings to my neighborhood. Communing close to home is part of an echo effect. When I commune in my yard or in a local park, I catch an echo of wilder nature. The miniature rock garden at the arboretum reminds my body of the alpine flower fields, and a sense of spaciousness washes through me. The smell of cedar relaxes my shoulder muscles and makes me smile, in part because it taps into memories of communing with cedars in a forest. The unconscious associations, the specific inspirations, and the new exercises I experience in wild areas all help me commune in my day-to-day life.

Thich Nhat Hanh is a Buddhist monk who was nominated for the Nobel Peace Prize by Martin Luther King, Jr. In his book *Peace Is Every Step,* Thich Nhat Hanh talks about the importance of leaving home from time to time:

As beginning meditators, we may want to leave the city and go off to the countryside to help close those windows that trouble our spirit. There we can become one with the quiet forest, and redis-cover and restore ourselves, without being swept away by the chaos of the "outside world." The fresh and silent woods help us remain in aware-ness, and when our awareness is well-rooted, and we can maintain it without faltering, we may wish to return to the city and remain there, less troubled.

I suggest adding to your yearly schedule two kinds of com-muning trips away from home. First, go to wild areas as unpopulated as possible: state parks, national parks, wildlife preserves, and national forests. Spend several days or more. Gradually, you can drop your defenses and be touched by spaciousness and silence you won't find in your ordinary life. These experiences will refresh you and con-tinue to teach you once you are back home.

Second, take weekend trips to one natural area you can return to over and over so that it feels like a second home to you. I go to a cottage called Beachwood that is only two hours from my Seattle home. I have stayed there often enough now that I have my favorite communing spots for all kinds of weather. The trees, bird calls, and smells are so familiar that they put me into a communing frame of mind almost immediately, just by association with other visits.

Safety

One of my friends said, "I could never commune with nature in my local park; Central Park is full of muggers and rats." Another friend said, "I love to commune in Central Park; there are lots of natural nooks to choose from."

Obviously, everyone is not afraid of the same things or the same places. Your fears will interfere with the focused attention you need to commune, so pay attention to whatever specific, even eccentric, things you are afraid of.

You can start in your own yard, or on your porch, or in a friend's yard, if you are afraid of being alone in public parks. In some parks I feel perfectly safe, in others I make sure I am near a busy jogging path or parking lot. Turning my back to the joggers or putting a bush between myself and the parking lot can give me the balance of privacy and safety that I need. Sometimes I carry pepper spray, and I do know the basics of self-defense, but I don't go places where I expect to use either one. I want to start out with as much serenity as I can.

Sometimes I go with a friend or a group of friends and we spread out to give ourselves that same blend of privacy and safety while we all commune. Often my more athletic friends will leave me at my communing spot and go off for a jog. I then have the security of knowing someone will soon be back to check on me.

Most assaults occur between people who know each

other, and most assaults by strangers occur after the stranger has cased out the situation well. While the news headlines about random violence in public areas arouse some fear in me, the statistics are so low I rarely fear being alone in parks. Since the likelihood of being in an auto accident is much higher than the likelihood of being mugged, I should probably fear the drive home!

Some people fear silence, or boredom, or being alone. Others fear not being essential to some important job or not being in control of what happens next. Still others fear that uncomfortable feelings about their lives might surface if they slow down and pay attention. Communing is not just a quick one-way ticket to bliss; it's also a ticket to self-awareness and spiritual growth. Some of that awareness will include uncomfortable feelings, and some of that growth will come from overcoming fears.

The Essentials to Bring Along

There are no essentials. Hiking books often list "the ten essentials" you should take with you on a hike: compass, matches, etc. Since I often go no farther than fifty feet from my car, I don't have to carry anything with me at all. On the other hand, a few items definitely make me more comfortable. One in particular has come in handy so often I now facetiously call it my "one essential": a big plastic bag. I discovered the hard way how essential a plastic bag is.

One stunning summer morning at 4 A.M. I sauntered through the slumbering village of Harrison Hot Springs to the lakeshore. The sky and lake were pink, the mountains were lavender, and not a soul was in sight. I sat on the first bench I came to, and my pants soaked up the cold morning dew like a sponge. I jumped up; that wouldn't work. I strolled down the dock hoping to lie down with my face close to the shimmering water but, of course, the dock was covered with cold dew also. I couldn't go back to my camper and wake up my traveling companion again at that hour, so I resorted to scouting garbage cans to look for a clean plastic bag that could rescue my morning.

Since then, I never leave home without one plastic bag. It allows me to sit on a soggy mossy log, a muddy path, or a waterfall-sprayed boulder. With a bag, I can protect myself from dew or bird droppings on my local park bench.

Two plastic bags let me lie down on wet grass, dusty ledges, or forest duff that would stick to my clothes. On the walk back I can use one of the bags to pick up litter and feel like I'm contributing to this land I love. Bags let me extend the range of where and when I sit, giving me more chances to find peace and privacy.

Along with the "one essential," I often take some items that will protect me and some that will make me more comfortable. I almost always take the protections of sunblock, insect repellent, earplugs, and a sun visor. One little annoyance like mosquitoes or a floodlight slanting into your eyes or a noisy nearby picnic can ruin an entire adventure. Sometimes I also take the pepper spray and a raincoat.

I almost always take the comfort of snacks, water, tissues, an inflatable pillow, and a long knit scarf. The snacks, water, and tissues let me stay out as long as I want; the pillow and scarf let me make rocky ground or lumpy tree trunks into comfortable seats and backrests.

When you won't be walking far from your car, you can take anything along that you want. I sometimes take my beach chair or a foam pad when I want to be really at ease, or a hot water bottle and a blanket when it's chilly. You may not think you would ever take a beach chair communing, but it almost rates as an essential for me. I've taken mine up ski lifts and onto ferry decks, onto canyon rims and into playgrounds. It makes communing easier.

When considering what to pack, remember that comfort is important for communing. You don't want to tough it out, you want to relax as easily as possible. After you have discovered your own favorite items, stash them in a daypack or sack ready to go at a moment's notice. You never know when the clouds may suddenly part on a full-moon night.

Tips for Communing with Nature

1. When to commune: from dusk to dawn; midweek; during challenging or unusual weather; off-season; when you are rested, fed, and comfortable.

2. Where to commune:

   a. As close as possible to your home, work, and regular routes of travel: yards, parks, empty lots; balconies, roofs, platforms; bits of land near dead ends, churches, cemeteries, playgrounds; near natural sounds or behind hills that block noise.

   b. Away from home: quiet, spacious, unpopulated wild areas for an extended stay; a place you can visit regularly and become familiar with.

3. For safety: stay within calling range of friends, jogging routes, and populated parking lots or picnic areas; carry pepper spray; learn self-defense; have a friend come back to meet you.

4. For comfort take along: a large plastic bag or two; sunblock, insect repellent, sun hat or visor, raincoat, earplugs, snacks, water, tissues, inflatable pillow, and scarf; luxury items such as a beach chair, foam pad, blanket, and hot water bottle.

In this chapter, you will learn the fastest way to switch from your everyday "busy" mindset to a communing mindset: You will learn to lock your preoccupations away and turn your attention to what you hope to experience by communing.

2
GETTING READY

In his first book, *Nature*, Ralph Waldo Emerson encouraged working people to restore themselves by going outdoors:

> *To the body and mind which have been cramped by noxious work or company, nature is medicinal and restores their tone. The tradesman, the attorney comes out of the din and craft of the street, and sees the sky and the woods, and is a man again. In their eternal calm, he finds himself.*

It sounds easy doesn't it? Just walk out into the street and nature will automatically refresh you. Well, for most of us, it's often not that simple.

For instance, has this ever happened to you? You manage to carve time out of your busy schedule to stroll through a park. Ten minutes into your walk, you realize you can't remember anything you've seen, heard, or smelled because you've been thinking about work. It's a common scenario, and it happens to everyone. Even Thoreau, one of America's most famous nature lovers, wrote

> *I am alarmed when it happens that I have walked a mile into the woods bodily, without getting there in spirit. In my afternoon walk I would fain forget all my morning occupations and my obligations to society. But it sometimes happens that I cannot easily shake off the village. The thought of some work will run in my head and I am not where my body is,—I am out of my senses. In my walks I would fain return to my senses. What business have I in the woods, if I am thinking of something out of the woods?*

Of course, it's not just thoughts of work that keep us "out of our senses." A retired person can be just as preoccupied as an employed person. A mind can be full of all kinds of worries, conversations, plans for the future, and To-Do lists. Our minds can create movies in our heads of all the things that have happened or might happen. We can get so involved reacting to these mental pictures and scripts that we don't see the real world around us.

I call this worrying, planning mindset the "busyness" mindset. It likes to convince us that it is just taking care of the urgent business of our lives. But, in fact, it often creates busy work and mental busyness that keep our attention tied up even when we could be relaxing.

A busyness mindset thinks too fast to commune. It's always in a hurry. It jumps from thought to thought and from choice to choice. It convinces us there is too much to do and not enough time to do it in. How can we relax in the park when our busyness mindset is nagging us to get back to the really important tasks at home or work?

The communing mindset, on the other hand, notices what is around us. It smells and feels and sees and hears. It's sensual.

The communing mindset is sometimes silent. This internal silence allows us to rest and to connect with the silence of nature. It allows us to hear our deep inner voices.

The communing mindset focuses here and now, not on our future plans. It has time to relax.

If carrying our busy thoughts everywhere—even to nature—has become an unconscious habit, what can we do to leave those thoughts behind, so we can get to the woods in spirit? We can pack.

When I'm planning to leave Seattle to visit friends in Minnesota, I pack up my Seattle life before I go. I stop the mail delivery, unplug the computer, and stack my unfinished paperwork into a To-Do pile to await my return. When I'm planning to commune with nature, I pack up my busyness mindset and leave it behind.

How do you pack up a mindset? The very first step—

and the most important step—is to *decide* to pack it. That might sound easy and obvious, but if you're distracted and overwhelmed, you will find it a difficult step to take. Nevertheless, it's *the most essential step*. Ambivalence will sabotage your plans. You must put as much determination and single-mindedness into your decision as you can muster. Once you've firmly decided, there are several easy techniques you can use to do the actual packing.

Writing is a powerful tool. Before you leave home, or while you sit in your car at the arboretum parking lot, write down all the things you're leaving behind. For instance, you might write: "I'm leaving behind:

the fence repair	the argument with Sam
the surgery decision	the credit card worries
birthday plans	the knocking noise in the car
the beans to pick	the meeting at work

I promise to pick this list up and look at it at seven o'clock tonight when I'm home again. I'll think about these issues at that time."

For some reason, putting things in writing helps the brain trust that you really will come back and shoulder your responsibilities once again. When you write that you promise to look at this list at seven o'clock, you're providing even more reassurance to your internal worrier. (Make sure you keep your promise!)

If you don't like to write, you can say your list out loud. "I'm leaving these issues behind, and I'll pick them up on my way home: my presentation, worries about my sick cat, the carpenter ants. . . ." If you're driving, you can imagine tossing your words out the window and driving away from them.

You can also picture putting your concerns one at a time into a balloon. Then tie the imaginary balloon to the door of your house, or to the bumper of your car, or to a tree at the start of the path, and promise yourself you will pick it up after your time in nature.

Your goal is to get your preoccupations out in a concrete way so you can clearly and obviously leave them behind. You can use as much creativity as you want in the process. You can sing your worries or draw some representation of each one. You can symbolically put each concern inside a penny and pile the pennies on your kitchen table.

If you want to think about one particular subject while you're in nature, put that topic on a piece of paper and tuck it into your pocket. That will reassure your internal worrier that you won't forget the issue. After communing, you'll be able to think about it with a rested mind. Some communing techniques open up new ways of thinking about a problem and reveal solutions that wouldn't have occurred to you inside your home or workplace.

I must admit that I often try to avoid packing up my busyness mindset. I hope it will fade away without any effort on my part. Sometimes it does—if the worries are small enough, if the situations are not urgent, or if I'm not too caught up in the drama.

If ignoring doesn't work within the first ten minutes, however, it's probably not going to work at all. At that point, I have the choice of walking around tense and pre-occupied (which makes communing impossible), or of stopping in my tracks and giving my worries to the nearest rocks or trees.

I discovered this technique of giving my worries to trees one day when I went to the Washington Park Arboretum and hadn't packed up my busyness mindset in advance. It was much faster and more effective than I could possibly have imagined. In the following journal entry, I describe that discovery.

The arboretum is my "home park." Since it's only seven minutes from my house and office, I go there often and know certain nooks well enough to feel at home.

Washington Park Arboretum   May

I've come to the arboretum exhausted. Since I have more time than I usually do, I plop myself in the grass on my orange pad and take a catnap. I surface occasionally and register the soothing sounds of robins singing and the wind rustling big maple leaves high overhead, then I sink back into dreamless sleep.

As soon as I wake up, my brain comes back to full attention. The worries of the day crowd back in, and I know I might as well get up. There will be no more peaceful dozing for me today.

Even as I walk through the sweet smells and bracing wind, my mind won't let go. *Okay,* I tell my internal worrier, *I guess I'll have to take some time to get rid of these nagging thoughts.*

I always spend this time reluctantly; I resent the price in time and attention that my everyday life exacts from me. By now, though, I know that if I don't pay up front, I'll be harassed by worry pickpockets during my whole walk.

I face an old magnolia tree. "I'm going to pretend you are the new laptop computer I just ordered," I say to the gray-green trunk. "I'm afraid of you."

This is nothing new. For the past week, I've been struggling with the decision of whether or not to buy it. As I speak to the tree now, I expect my litany of laptop fears to pour out. Instead, my next sentence is, "I'm really excited about you. I think you'll add so much to my life. I can't wait to have you and start working on you."

I'm puzzled by my own words. I throw in some fears; I'm doing this exercise to name and exorcise my concerns, after all. "I'm worried I won't be able to figure out your programming. I'm worried about the time it will take to learn you." My speech is half-hearted. My feelings have really switched over to excitement. Okay then, "I'm really excited about you," I say with a sigh and move on.

A cedar trunk gets the book I'm ghostwriting. Again, words I don't expect pour out, "I'm really excited about you, too. What a great opportunity to work on something I believe in. I like having a challenging project on my agenda." That's it. I'm dumbfounded. I move on.

"But I'm trying to dump worries!" I say. I sit on a bench surrounded by rhododendron bushes. I give each bush a category of worries. "You are the endless house repairs. You are the van repairs. You are my piles of mail." There. I don't feel excitement about those at all. On the other hand, I don't feel the panicked worrying I usually feel when I think about them either. I just feel weary.

I watch the white blossoms and glossy leaves on each of my worry bushes bob in the wind. I take a deep breath. I relax.

I'm not sure this is working. I expected to have a big emotional outpouring of fears; instead, my worries are turning into simple excitement or weariness.

A maple trunk gets my sister's visit, a fir trunk gets a friend's visit. They are both events I'm looking forward to, but I don't want to think about them while I'm in the park.

I've run out of worries. I assume I haven't focused well enough to release my feelings, but I continue my walk, permeated by a gentle excitement.

I walk through the trees, past the visitor center, and out to the marsh walk. I keep expecting my worries to surface, but every time I try to think about them, they literally feel as though they are behind me in a separate reality. I meander through a world filled only with wind and smiles.

I don't stop to commune because this walk is just for exercise, but even without meditating, my attention stays present. My thighs burn a little; the sun blares in my eyes as the trail turns. Muscles, sun, wind, waving leaves, and birdsongs make up my reality.

On the way back to the car, I walk past the blooming rhododendrons. I'm still relaxed. I pass the maple and the fir, the cedar and the magnolia. When I return to the car, I have to remind myself what's on my list of concerns. I'm surprised to feel no tension as I run through the list. I feel only refreshed.

I often assume that dealing with my pile of concerns will take a lot of time and energy and ruin my visit with nature. But actually, my worries usually pour out pretty easily. My conversation with the trees and bushes, for instance, took only ten minutes. I had plenty of time left over to enjoy the arboretum. I also had a relaxed body and mind.

Naming my fears one by one, and giving each one to a different tree or bush, changed them from a huge, overwhelming mass to discrete problems I could get my mind around. Each one was as concrete as a tree, with a beginning and an end. I could look at them—and even touch them—one at a time.

Putting my worries outside of myself—literally getting some distance from them—relaxed me immediately. As I gave each bush a worry, the tension from that issue left my body.

Throughout this exercise, I faced a dilemma you might run into when you want to commune with nature: What if something you want to do makes you look silly? Talking to trees looks silly, for instance. Should I have restrained myself? Should I have done something more adult and proper?

I think most of us have at least one old wound from a time when we were called ridiculous or stupid. We remember with terror the judgment of our peers, even if they can't do anything to us now.

So it takes courage to look silly—yet that's what

communing with nature may require of us. It may not demand the bravery to fight a mountain lion or to scale a sheer rock face. But it may require the courage to face our worries and the willingness to do things other adults might consider offbeat.

At the arboretum, I didn't solve any of the individual problems I was worried about, though I could have stopped and worked on them if I had wanted to. I could also have stopped and communed with nature at a deeper level. Instead, I solved what was the most pressing problem of the moment; I became free enough of anxious feelings and nagging thoughts to enjoy my walk.

Often, once I've switched off my busyness mindset, I can stride into the park with a mind that's empty and receptive and ready to commune. Sometimes, however, my mind keeps filling that space with irrelevant chatter. When that happens, I need to take some specific actions to turn on my communing mindset. My first step is to direct my mind toward what I'm looking for.

I ask myself, *Why am I coming to nature today? What do I hope will happen?*

Just as I listed my concerns and left them behind, I can list my goals for going to nature. I can write them, or speak them aloud, or visualize them. I can sing them, or draw them, or bring along an object that symbolizes them. It's easier to get control of my thinking if I deliberately choose a new topic for my brain to consider.

Stating my goals helps me not only get into a communing mindset, but into a communing "bodyset." My muscles relax and my breathing slows when I say a phrase such as, "I want to be empty, silent, still, receptive." My skin tingles and my ears start scanning when I say, "I want to get out of my head and into my senses."

Sometimes my mind is so tired or overwhelmed on a particular day that I can't remember why I'm going to nature. Then I like to read something that will put me into a communing frame of mind. I read spiritual quotes or nature writing I've collected, or I read one of my own journal entries.

Over the years, I've collected some of my favorite goals into a reminder list I've entitled, "Before I Enter Nature I Want to Remember . . ." This poem/list is very effective for me because the ideas come from my own experiences. Some phrase in the poem will evoke a memory or a sensation that helps me get on track.

You may want to collect some nature poems or sayings that touch you. And write your own! Until then, try using mine.

Before I Enter Nature
I Want to Remember . . .

I come here
   To get out of my head and into my senses

   To immerse myself in peace and beauty

   To feel kinship with life

   To feel at home

I come here
   To be empty

                silent

                     still

                          receptive

I come here
   To be changed:
         to get a new perspective
               to find an answer
                     to heal a wound
                          to learn

I come here
   To be wild

         To be engulfed by wildness
                     and mystery
                          and wonder

I come here
    To worship
            to thank
                    to praise
                            to love

Another way to switch into a communing mindset is to pray. Praying is not just a traditional religious practice, it is a powerful way to reset your mental and emotional focus.

As assistant crown attorney in northern Canada, Rupert Ross was caught off guard when he first heard Native people offer an opening prayer before a court proceeding. He didn't see the connection between justice issues and prayer. He writes

> As I listened closely to both the words and the commitment of the prayer-givers, however, I began to feel differently. Those prayers regularly recite our commonality as human beings struggling to find ways to work towards common goals. They ask for assistance in reminding everyone present of their good fortune to live on such a wonderful planet and with such wonderful gifts. They ask that we remember to treat each other, and the planet, respectfully. I can honestly say that I have

been moved many times. I have seen the same reaction from other white people, including bureaucrats, politicians, and hard-bitten police-men. What I sense we are moved towards is a rededication of our minds and spirits. The day's activities will not just involve the business *of the day's topic, but the* growth *of all people there.*

In short, I am beginning to agree with the tra-ditional Native conviction that until each person's mental or spiritual state has been addressed, the time cannot be right to begin the day's particular activity. Minds preoccupied with other issues or full of negative feelings carried over from other contexts will contaminate the proceedings.

You don't have to pray to any particular deity or pantheon of deities. When you pray you can simply state your hopes and intentions and place your communing into a larger context. If you do have a relationship with a particular deity or pantheon, praying opens you to receiving help and guidance from that source.

When you switch from a busyness mindset to a com-muning mindset you are doing more than just changing your intentions or the topic you want your mind to think about. You are changing the *way* your brain is working.

One way to picture this switch from a busyness mindset to a communing mindset is to imagine you're taking control from one half of your brain and giving it to the other half. Researchers have discovered that the two hemispheres of your cerebrum control different activities and use different thinking processes. The left hemisphere is usually in charge of your workaday life; it controls rational, logical, and verbal thinking. The right hemisphere of your brain, on the other hand, uses the intuitive, creative, and holistic thinking processes that are essential for communing.

So when you use a visualization like putting your concerns into a balloon, you're activating the creative side of your brain. When you read the words of my poem or write your own goals, you again access your right hemisphere because you feel the emotions in the poem, like kinship and at-homeness, which are experienced through the right hemisphere.

In his book *What the Buddha Never Taught*, Tim Ward describes what the switch from left brain to right brain is like when it happens during meditation:

> *The left hemisphere is the dominant partner in most human activities; it seldom relinquishes its control. It thrives on complex tasks and if not fully taxed, will wander distractedly. The right brain is easily absorbed with just the sort of simple activities the left side finds tedious. For example, if required to concentrate on the mundane simplicity of breathing, the left brain will rebel. It will want to think of something more*

interesting. But if attention is continually returned to breathing, the left may eventually give control to the right brain. When this happens, a distinct mental shift will be experienced. Restlessness will cease as the right brain takes over. A person in this condition will relax into peaceful contemplation. Viewed in this way, meditation is a therapy for lessening left brain dominance. As the passive right brain learns how to be in control, enabling us to lead more creative and intuitive lives, this restores a balance in our own human nature.

When Tim Ward meditates, he continually returns his attention to his breathing. When you want to don a communing mindset, return your attention to your reasons for communing.

To commune with nature, the single most important thing you can do is *decide* to commune. If you can put a strong, single-minded determination into that decision, you're halfway to your goal. Packing up your busyness mindset and switching to a communing mindset will be easy or difficult in direct proportion to the strength of your decision. Once you've decided, packed, and turned your thoughts toward communing, the next step is pure pleasure: settling in.

Tips for Getting Ready

1. Decide to commune.
2. Spill out your worries and To-Do lists: Write them, say them, draw them, sing them, or picture them vividly in your mind and imagine stuffing them in a balloon. Give them one at a time to different pennies or trees or flowers.
3. Leave those contents where you can come back to them.
4. Promise yourself you will deal with the issues later. Give yourself a specific time if you can.
5. If you want to work on a particular issue after you're refreshed, write down that topic and tuck it in your pocket.
6. Write, say aloud, or picture what you want from your time in nature today. If you can't think of anything, read the poem/list in this book or a poem you write yourself.
7. When a worry intrudes during your time in nature, remind yourself you've promised to come back to it, and then push it out of your mind. If it's a concern you haven't written on your list yet, write it on a slip of paper.

In order to experience nature deeply, you need a calm mind and a relaxed body. Even though you have left your busyness mindset behind, your body may still be tense. In this chapter, you will learn how to use stillness, boundary-setting, and relaxation techniques to help you settle in.

3
SETTLING IN

Joseph Campbell, the renowned mythologist, could have been talking about communing when he wrote

> People say that what we're all seeking is a meaning for life. . . . I think that what we're seeking is an experience of being alive, so that our life experiences on the purely physical plane will have resonances within our own innermost being and reality, so that we actually feel the rapture of being alive.

Communing helps us feel the rapture of being alive. Notice Campbell doesn't use the words "think about" or "realize"; he says "feel."

We are communing when we *feel* something in response

to what we're experiencing: We feel exhilarated or awestruck or serene. We can watch the most spectacular sunset in the world, but unless we have a physical and emotional reaction, we're not communing.

Since communing requires a physiological response, bodies that are tied up in knots of anxiety can't do it. The sensations of communing, which are generally more subtle than anxiety, won't have much impact on tight muscles and organs. I don't know anyone who can feel both peaceful and tense at the same time.

When we think about communing with nature, we usually picture ourselves sitting in pristine, silent wilderness at the end of a long trail. We've had a whole day to unwind, or a whole weekend to sink into the gentle rhythms of the natural world. We easily and spontaneously relax and slow down.

This is a lovely fantasy and sometimes it comes true. Having time away from the noises and demands of everyday life, and being surrounded by nothing but beauty and magnificence, can be very calming. On the other hand, we may be preoccupied with our aching feet, we may be having a fantasy argument with the people who clear-cut that last stretch of trail, or we may be worried about finding the next campsite. Wilderness does not guarantee relaxation. In any case, if we want a consistent relationship with nature, we will be spending most of our communing time closer to home where we will definitely have to make conscious efforts to settle in—and relax.

I used to deny myself the refreshment and inspiration of communing with nature because I thought I didn't have enough time. Once you've mastered these settling-in techniques you can get to a rejuvenating level of communing in less than half an hour. If you're worried about taking time away from being productive, remember that time spent communing with nature will leave you clearer and more energetic for whatever work still lies ahead in your day. According to stress expert Larry Dossey, M.D., author of *Recovering the Soul,* "Studies show that when people have time to relax, they actually are able to achieve more."

Because settling in seems like a simple concept, you may be tempted to underestimate the effect it can have. Without using any other communing exercises, you can have powerful experiences just by settling in.

Franz Kafka, the Austrian philosopher and poet, describes the power of the settling-in process like this:

> *You need not leave your room. Remain sitting at your table and listen. You need not even listen, simply wait. You need not even wait, just learn to become quiet, and still, and solitary. The world will freely offer itself to you to be unmasked. It has no choice; it will roll in ecstasy at your feet.*

Most of us can't get from our habitual state of tension and worry to Kafka's state of quiet and stillness very quickly unless we help ourselves with some settling-in techniques.

In the following journal entry, I employ several techniques in quick succession because I have limited time. Using a still object, thought-stopping, deep breathing, counting backwards, and saying calming words each help me relax more deeply. I will explain each of these in detail after the journal excerpt.

While you are reading the journal entry, challenge yourself to let go and experience it. Slow down, switch over to your right brain, and let your senses react. Then the next time you go to nature to commune, you will have body memories and right-brain memories to draw upon.

Throughout the book, as I switch from logical explanations to experiential journal entries, you will be making the same switch from a busyness mindset to a communing mindset. You will have to make this switch yourself when you go to nature. Practice here. Let the entries help you. You will notice if you try to read the journal entries fast without giving yourself time to respond to them, you may feel a little oV-center or Xat. If you take time to relax into them, you will feel refreshed.

Washington Park Arboretum   January
    I have taken my aerobic walk through the arbore-
    tum and, although I have only twenty more min-
    utes, I want to find some peace here. I get my beach
    chair from the van and set it in a grassy spot behind
    several large bushes.

This is not an ordinary nook in the arboretum. This is right next to the major road and parking lot. Traffic noise is roaring twenty yards away. Can I commune here? Can I commune with so little time?

My grassy area is splashed with sunlight. Bare branches stand dark and still against the green blades. The few leaves left hanging, brown and curled, are completely motionless. I try to match their stillness. My skin feels as though its cells are realigning and relaxing as the calmness of the scene before me sinks in.

Even with this great role model of stillness, my mind keeps racing over this morning's conversations. *Slow down!* I shout to myself in my brain.

I close my eyes and take three slow deep breaths. My shoulder muscles relax and my skin tingles as tension drains from me with each exhale. I count slowly from five to zero. With each count I imagine myself taking a step down a dark staircase into deeper relaxation. My face muscles hang lax. My chest muscles, hands, and internal organs all let go.

Suddenly a strange sensation washes through me; I feel as though I'm in a world completely separate from the traffic-filled world twenty yards away. Here, in my little niche, all is still and quiet. In that world over there, everything is noisy and rushing. I feel like an anachronism, like an old woman basking on her frontier porch while a freeway buzzes nearby. In my world, nothing needs to happen as fast as whatever is going on in that one. In fact, nothing needs to happen here at all.

I go deeper inside, deeper into the "doing nothing." I feel very relaxed. I touch the bottom of doing nothing. It's like touching my foot to the ground. "Nothing" is very solid. "Nothing" is secure and comforting.

Some part of me that's still awake in this trance perceives a different and very foreign way of being in life. *Before you can do something,* it says, *you must be able to do nothing. The something that you do must be a choice springing from the rightness of doing nothing.*

I savor the words. "Before you can do something, you must be able to do nothing." It sounds so simple. I luxuriate in the feeling of doing nothing, thinking nothing, feeling only stillness.

You must be able to do nothing, I repeat silently. With each repetition of those words, I become even more still and relaxed inside. What if this were not a temporary trip, but a lifestyle? What if a culture valued this level of deep inner peace and stillness? What if we were instructed as children to take no actions and to set no goals unless they sprung from this place, unless they were clearly choices instead of habits or obligations? I can almost imagine it.

I surface slowly, savoring the feeling, not just of doing nothing, but of valuing doing nothing. For just a little while, doing nothing has been center stage.

I open my eyes to the solid, motionless scene before me: grass, leaves, arching branches. There is not the slightest breeze. Nothing, precious nothing, is happening.

It's certainly possible to commune while moving. Thoreau is famous for communing while walking. And after breaking the four-minute mile, Roger Bannister said, "No longer conscious of my movement, I discovered a new unity with nature. I had found a new source of power and beauty, a source I never dreamt existed."

Despite Thoreau's and Bannister's mobile success, my most profound communing experiences occur when I'm completely still. Before I begin communing, I may have to stretch or walk in order to release excess energy or unkink knotted muscles, but stillness is my goal.

Stillness allows me to slow down. Stillness frees up my attention so I can focus on what I'm feeling. In his book on mindfulness meditation, Jon Kabat-Zinn describes elegantly why we need to be still:

> *. . . we have got to pause in our experience long enough to let the present moment sink in; long enough to actually* feel *the present moment, to see it in its fullness, to hold it in awareness and thereby come to know and understand it better.*

At the arboretum, I started settling in by trying to match the stillness of dead leaves. Quieting my body didn't stop my mind, however, so I employed a technique called thought-stopping. To use thought-stopping, simply shout in your mind, *Stop!* or *Slow down!* Then redirect your thoughts. It may sound silly, but if you're persistent, it works. Stephen Levine suggests a gentler approach in his meditation book *A Gradual Awakening:* just note your thought by silently saying "thinking," and then bring your attention back to your focus.

Often you can relax enough by taking three slow deep breaths. Never underestimate the power of breathing. In fact, you can take three slow deep breaths anytime during your workday and keep your tension level down. Start your inhale by pushing out the lowest part of your abdomen, then let the breath fill your belly and chest. When you exhale, pay attention to the feeling of your muscles relaxing. Pause at the end of the exhale to relish the delightful looseness. This is the moment during which your muscles can relax most completely.

Notice the tension level in your body right now. On a scale from zero to ten, if zero is completely relaxed and ten is completely tense, what number would you rate yourself? Now take three slow deep breaths and rate yourself again. Using this forty-five second exercise, most people decrease their tension level several numbers.

The exercise of counting down from five to zero is one of many quick-relaxation techniques. I've listed others in the tips at the end of the chapter. Once you get comfortable using them, you will notice all kinds of situations where a short break with a quick-relaxation exercise will increase your pleasure, alertness, and productivity. While you might think that relaxing would put you to sleep, it actually releases energy you have tied up in your muscles so you have more vitality. Relaxing is a skill like any other. The more you practice, the more quickly your body will respond.

In the arboretum, once I was still enough to pay close attention, and relaxed enough for my muscles to respond, I discovered words I resonated to. Repeating those words, because they were calming words, deepened my relaxation even further. Sometimes I start the settling-in process by repeating soothing words such as "let go," "be still," or "peace."

In the next experience, I use another important settling-in technique: setting a boundary. Most of us have what I call "choosing disorders." We have trouble choosing one thing to do because we think we should be able to see and do everything. We hate to say no or limit ourselves, so we end up frantic and fragmented, always trying to do too much. Setting a boundary breaks this pattern. Setting a boundary says, "I choose this."

May

Beaver Pond Conservation Area near Bellingham, Washington

I have twenty minutes. Part of my Nature Conservancy field-trip group is slogging around the beaver pond, the other part is walking up the hill and back. When I was told I could spend this time any way I wanted, I said I'd just sit here on this log, thank you very much. We're to be back at the cars in half an hour.

It's hard to center. The Nature Conservancy annual meeting this morning hit me like a brick. It's one thing to suspect that the wilderness is vanishing; it's another to hear an expert say The Nature Conservancy is going to have to find another focus for the next ten years because there won't be any wilderness in Washington State left to save.

I spread sheets of writing paper across the moist moss that carpets a downed log, and sit on them. The log itself stretches out into the bog like a pathway into another world. With only twenty minutes, I don't have time to drift into quiet; I have to push myself there.

I decide to do a quick 4-3-2-1 self-hypnosis exercise: name four sights, four sounds, and four physical sensations; then name three of each, then two of each, then one.

"Four: I see the blue sky, I see the tall fir, I see the undulating water, I see the wet moss.

    I hear the wind in the trees, I hear the fading voices of the people on the field trip, I hear a bird chirp, I hear my own exhales.

    I feel my hand on my knee, I feel the warm sun on my arm, I feel my chest rising and falling, I feel my face muscles relaxing.

Three: I see the water plants, I see sparkles on the water, I see my foot.

    I hear a fly buzzing, I hear a duck splash, I hear myself swallow.

    I feel my foot pressing against the log, I feel heavy, I feel my shoulders relaxing.

Two: I see the water resting against the log, I see dead bark.

    I hear the wind, I hear a crow call.

    I feel my arms against my body, I feel my eyelids close when I blink.

One: I see grass.

    I hear the ringing in my ears.

    I feel a relaxed heaviness through my whole body."

I take a deep breath. Now I am more present. My heavy body feels connected to the ground here. My senses are alert.

I know that I won't be able to see everything or commune with everything in twenty minutes. Looking around is too uncentering. I have to set a boundary. So I imagine myself in the middle of a big bubble that encloses a twenty-five-foot circle of bog, and I call this my home. Ah, yes, that feels better. When I keep my attention inside my little dome, I become even calmer.

Finally I close my eyes and visualize the spiritual core I imagine lives near my heart. I set it free to fill the bubble. Now my surroundings are part of me— water shimmers in my chest, rushes stand tall inside me. The energy they emanate glows inside my own trunk.

There is a sudden clarity to everything within this larger circle of me. I look down and watch a tadpole wiggle against the log. It's so chubby it looks pregnant. Every detail of its body stands out as though it were under a magnifying glass. I can almost feel the slide of water against my own body as its tail wriggles in constant S's.

All the agitation has drained out of me. I'm happy to focus on the few feet right below me. I feel as though I could watch the tadpole forever, but other things are too curious to ignore. Big beetle-like bugs paddle underwater on invisible freeways, each one using a bubble of air as if it were an Aqua Lung. I can see their skinny black legs reach and push as they stroke.

All the creatures in this little world are intent on the urgencies of their lives. How strange that all this drama goes on outside my knowledge most of the time. Fifteen minutes ago I stood on this log with twelve people and gazed across the water at the osprey and dead trees, oblivious to the water bugs.

Water droplets balance on the leaves of plants that vine across the surface of the water. How did the plants catch those gems? It hasn't rained in days. Did a duck splash the water up? Did the leaves hoard the droplets from this morning's dew? How little I know of the basics of life here.

Twenty minutes with nature, inside a boundary that limits and focuses my attention, are enough. These tadpoles, these beetles, and these droplets on leaves are enough. I can relax into being with them, knowing that this level of communion will refresh me more than twenty minutes of stalking up and down the path collecting images. This peace and this shimmering sunlight can seep into my soul and give me a place to return to when I need it. I feel like one of the leaves that has captured a droplet, only my droplet is made of beauty. Just one droplet in my heart is plenty.

At Beaver Pond I had as short a time to commune as I had on my visit to the arboretum, so I started out by deciding to commune; then I settled in by relaxing and setting a boundary. At the arboretum, I sat in a nook that had a natural boundary: bushes and a grassy area limited my focus. At Beaver Pond, I had to create a boundary artificially so I wouldn't get overwhelmed with choices. Limiting your choices and the input you receive is automatically calming.

I created a boundary at Beaver Pond in two ways: I imagined a bubble that encompassed a small area around me, and I did the self-hypnosis exercise. The 4-3-2-1 self-hypnosis exercise did more than just relax me. It engaged my senses instead of my thinking brain, and it made me focus on one thing at a time. Each series of seeing, hearing, and feeling focused my awareness on my immediate body sensations. My awareness was limited and slowed. I settled in even more quickly by mentioning the sensations of relaxing, like "I feel my shoulders relaxing, I feel heavy."

Sometimes this exercise relaxes me too much and I feel as though I am sinking into a deep trance. When I commune I want to be relaxed but still alert.

Try the 4-3-2-1 exercise right now and see how it works for you. It will take about two minutes to see, hear, and feel the ten different sensations the exercise requires. If you can't hear ten different sounds in your vicinity, you can repeat things you've already mentioned. You will be surprised how relaxed you can get in two minutes!

Decide to commune, be still, put away your busyness mindset, relax, create a boundary, and see what happens next. These deceptively simple steps are so effective you often won't need to do more.

Tips for Settling In

1. Decide to commune.
2. Be still. Use something still in your surroundings as a role model.
3. Use thought-stopping to set aside your busyness mindset.
4. Take three slow deep breaths.
5. Repeat any relaxing phrase that comes to mind as you're communing.
6. Find or create a boundary and keep your awareness inside it.
7. Do a relaxation exercise:

    a. Count slowly from five to zero. With each number, let go of more tension. You can release more overall tension with each number, or you can move from the outer layer of skin, through layers of muscles, to the center of your internal organs and bones. Zero is total relaxation.

b. Do fifteen seconds of slow stretches. Particularly stretch your neck and shoulders.

c. Imagine tension draining from the top of your head all the way down and out your fingers and toes. Give it a color and watch it flow down your face and neck, down your arms, down your shoulders and chest and back and pelvis, down your organs and spine, down your legs. Feel your muscles relax as it flows by.

d. Imagine you are a cup of water and relaxation is a drop of ink that falls into you. Watch and feel the drop as it slowly disperses through your body.

e. Close your eyes and say relaxing words to yourself slowly. My favorites are: "Drain . . . relax . . . be still . . . soften . . . let go . . . go deeper . . . breathe."

f. Imagine you are a cloud. Feel the warm sun on your back. Be aware of the spaces between your water droplets. Float.

g. Use the 4-3-2-1 self-hypnosis exercise. Say four things you see, hear, and sense physically. Then say three of each, then two of each, then one of each.

In this chapter, you will discover the power of experiencing nature directly, without the mediating effect of words. When you're silent, you can be receptive, passive, and wide open.

You can use silence to help you settle in, or you can use it to take you to a state of deeper relaxation and sharper awareness after you've settled in. This chapter will teach you how to use breathing, listening, slow motion, and sensory awareness to reach and maintain a silent state of mind.

4
USING SILENCE

Most of us don't have much experience with silence. We may lock our doors and close our windows to shut out the racket from the streets, but then we turn on the television or the radio. On the occasions when we do turn off the sound system in the living room, we discover that we still have a radio announcer chattering away inside our own heads.

Many years ago, I was reading some literature from Alcoholics Anonymous and a phrase jumped out at me: What's the point of praying if you don't take the time to listen for a reply? Good point, I thought. So I sat still and tried to be silent for one minute and just listen.

I couldn't do it. My mind kept wandering. I couldn't believe it. I tried again. I still couldn't make it all the way to a minute.

Over the years since then, I've tried to silence my mind in order to listen to nature. I've discovered some techniques that make it easier to have a quiet mind, and I've discovered how powerful silence is.

Being silent is one of the best ways to begin or deepen a visit with nature, because it helps me settle in and be receptive. Once I decide to be silent, I'm no longer in charge. I will listen, not speak. I will follow, not lead. I'll be a satellite dish, not a broadcast tower. Rabbi Dov Baer, a great teacher of mysticism in the Hasidic school, once wrote: "You must be nothing but an ear which hears what the universe of the word is saying in you. The moment you hear what you yourself are saying, you must stop."

Silence clears the thoughts off the neural freeways in my brain so the sounds and smells and sights of nature can flow in. Silence also clears the neural freeways through the muscles and organs in the rest of my body, which is usually kept so busy reacting to my thoughts it barely registers the wealth of sensations in the world around it. Silence creates an internal emptiness.

When I'm silent and receptive, I'm asking myself to

make a 180-degree turn from my daily habits. In my every-day life, I'm in charge and always thinking; passive is a dirty word. In nature, passive is an essential word. Nature will rarely push through the verbal walls I build around myself; I must create an opening myself.

Luther Burbank, an early twentieth-century scientist who produced over 800 new varieties of plants through hybridization, gave this advice to anyone who wanted to learn from nature:

> *Preconceived notions, dogmas, and all personal prejudice and bias must be laid aside. Listen patiently, quietly and reverently to the lessons, one by one, which Mother Nature has to teach. . . . She conveys her truths only to those who are passive and receptive.*

You don't need to go to the wilderness to be silent with nature. The grammar school playground five blocks from my house has a wonderful jungle gym with climbing chains, broad platforms, and slides. One morning before children arrived, I perched on a platform and communed with nature in silence. Two things aided me that often help when communing in town: it was early enough that other people weren't around yet, and I had my "one essential"— the big plastic bag I can put down to protect me from wet or muddy spots.

Leschi School   November

It's early enough that the grass is still wet and there's a chill to the air. Looking for a drier place to settle in, I climb the jungle gym and spread my plastic bag on the damp wooden platform at the top.

I read for a while, then lie back to rest. Suddenly my entire world is a bright blue sky studded with white puff clouds. Delighted, I decide to take a minute of internal silence. I count twelve breaths slowly, in and out, in and out, trying to relax into the big blue silence.

It isn't as hard to be quiet as it often is. My busy-ness mindset isn't in full swing yet, and I've spent the last half hour reading some of my old journal entries that describe communing experiences I had last spring. Those always help me center.

Twelve breaths is a long time. In the silence, I first notice the rush of sensations around me: cool gusts of air on my face, rattling leaves, singing robins, and the smell of wet grass. I'm amazed at the richness I had been blocking out when I was focused on reading.

Next I'm aware of the internal sensations of muscles relaxing, body softly rocking, and heart thumping. I let go into the soft sensation of not trying. Gently, the life force surrounds and fills me.

Usually I have to be silent before I can feel connected to the life force. Rarely does the life force interrupt my chattering mind to connect with me.

Taking twelve breaths in total silence sounds easy, doesn't it? It's not, believe me. But try it for yourself right now. Put this book on your lap and try to take twelve breaths without thinking a thought. It will take about a minute.

To achieve a quiet mind, meditation teachers often suggest that you notice how your breath feels as it passes the tip of your nose. This gives you a nonverbal focus for your attention so your mind can settle down.

When I do that, I can concentrate easily on the inhale and the exhale. They produce tickles and rocking and whispers of sound to entertain my mind. But in the still moment after the exhale, thoughts jump into the gap and take my mind off on some tangent.

So I make it a point to focus on that gap. I either count my breaths and say the number during that space, or I concentrate on the feeling of stillness and the sound of silence I find there. To keep my mind quiet in that resting spot is my only goal.

Now the inhale and exhale are almost superfluous. I wait through them for the delicious bit of silence in between. I notice the sound and feel the rocking of my breaths. Then

I settle into the stillness that feels like my real home.

In *The Tibetan Book of Living and Dying,* Sogyal Rinpoche describes the space between breaths like this:

> *Each time you breathe out, and before you breathe in again, you will find that there will be a natural gap, as the grasping dissolves.*
>
> *Rest in that gap, in that open space. And when, naturally, you breathe in, don't focus especially on the inbreath but go on resting your mind in the gap that has opened up.*

According to meditation teachers, even experienced meditators usually have to wade through five to fifteen minutes of mental garbage before they can settle into periods of silence. What a relief to hear that! I had worried that my busy mind meant I was particularly neurotic. Now it simply means that to get a minute of silence, I'll probably have to persevere for five to fifteen minutes.

So when I sit down to be silent with nature, I often start by counting one hundred breaths. That allows time for the mental dust to settle. Even in wild natural areas, where I hope it will be easy to be silent, I often have to put forth effort to quiet my mind.

Banff National Park, Alberta, Canada   July

I've set my beach chair at the edge of Upper
Waterfowl Lake. I'm listening to the melodies of the
lake and birds through the static of the traffic.
Sometimes I can hear waterfalls humming down
Mount Chephren during a break in the passing
cars.

A loon calls from the far end of the lake. Small
birds chitter and cry behind me. I suddenly remember what my friend Liz said when I asked her what
she does when she wants to commune with nature.
"I listen," she said.

The lake quiets. Ripples glide toward me and
slide onto the beach soundlessly. The wind blows
against the back of my head and against the incoming waves, dimpling their smoothness.

My partner, Sandra Jo, walks up the beach to
meet me with her florescent-pink beach chair in
tow. We chat about how to marinate tofu and how
she will sculpt the next fountain she plans. Then she
says, "Teach me a communing exercise."

"Here's one I use sometimes," I say. "Count your
breaths, saying the number in your mind at the end
of the exhale. Try to keep your mind free of other
thoughts as you count. Keep your eyes closed for
the first ten counts, then open them for the next ten
counts. Close them for the next ten counts, and so

on. When you reach one hundred, stop counting your breaths and just try to keep a silent mind."

As I close my eyes to count, I'm most strongly aware of the wind buffeting my neck. It changes directions like a boxer. When I get to the number ten and open my eyes, I can see rain pouring on the peaks to either side of us. A sound like thunder echoes across the lake. A loon cries.

I close my eyes and sink into the world of patting wind and rumbling traffic sounds. When I open my eyes, I count one peak for each breath, starting with the most distant ones and moving to the nearer ones. I watch the rain clouds and rippling water.

By the third time I open my eyes, I'm ready to stop *looking* at the sights. I merely rest my eyes on the scene; I let it all in at once without reaching for it. The view is a mandala cut in half. The bottom half holds rippling turquoise, the top half holds gray peaks in a cloud-dotted sky.

My breath comes more slowly and I relax more deeply. It seems hard to close my eyes and keep them closed.

As the number one hundred arrives, I taste a sweet silence that's more than silence. It's as though by being silent I'm joining the land in its own language of silence. Even when I worry what weather the wind is blowing in from behind me, it's the silence between the words in my mind that I'm aware of.

I find myself breathing more quietly, more gently, not wanting even that small whoosh to disturb my awareness of the greater breathing and silence around me. I'm listening again, as I did when I first arrived, but it feels different now. I'm not listening for sounds. I'm part of the silence the sounds float through.

The wind sings through the spruce trees behind me. Tiny droplets speckle my hands. Still, I'm aware of the underlying silence. Silence hangs beneath and between each sound, like the white page that lies beneath and between printed words. Swallows swoop over the lake; a blackbird pecks along the shore; ripples slide up the gravel beach—all in silence.

We meditate for twenty minutes. When we finish, Sandra Jo says, "It was a success! I didn't lose the count, and at one hundred it was easier to be in silence or to bring myself back to silence. After I got to one hundred, I wasn't in a hurry for it to be over. It was harder when my eyes were open, but the alternating kept me focused."

I tell her, "I think I made up this communing exercise because I can't bear to be in a beautiful place without looking at it. But I can't meditate deeply with my eyes open either. It's a compromise."

When I'm silent long enough, and stay alert enough, something unusual happens. I go beyond being receptive—I join with nature. I get a feeling of at-oneness where nature and I are the same. My air and its air are the same. The stuff of me and the stuff of nature are the same.

I join nature by using its primary language—silence. I join it by removing the artificial barriers that words and analyses throw up between us.

In the *Banff National Park Newsletter,* R. W. Sanford describes the experience of silence-induced union like this:

> *In the silences between the river's murmured phrases, I seek a brief moment of union when the universe focuses sharply on me and I stare timidly back at the tiny image I make on the mirror of its conscious eye. Time and rock and ice merge and inner and outer worlds are, at last, as one. The value of this wilderness resides in the power of this brief union to make me whole.*

Sometimes I don't use a specific exercise to get to silence. As the next experience illustrates, if I put enough determination behind the decision to be silent, that decision itself can be enough. I work at being silent, and in the process I find things that help: breathing with my mouth open, moving slowly, and gazing at the spaces between things.

Point Defiance Park, Tacoma, Washington   November

My life has been so busy and noisy lately, I need to come to the park to quiet down. First, I take a brisk walk for fifteen minutes. I can't do more than that because of my recently sprained ankle. I stop before a giant maple decked out with lush moss and delicate ferns and tell myself to keep my mind silent. I breathe softly. I can feel my heart pounding and my muscles relaxing.

The maple is silent also. A few yellow leaves bob gently on one of its lower branches, but they don't make a sound. Shadows play across its trunk in complete quiet. The cool air is thick with the scent of sweet cedar and decaying leaves.

I can hear a bird flutter overhead and the tap of one leaf as it hits the ground. I begin to walk in slow motion. Each footstep crunches on the carpet of leaves as I push through the thick silence.

I stop again when my face is inches from a cedar frond that is dangling from a long strand of spider's silk. It twists and rocks in a breeze too gentle for my skin to register. I blow on it. My breath is loud. The frond dances wildly in complete silence.

By standing in silence and walking in silence, I feel as though I've merged with the air and with the life force. The silence of the air flows through my chest and my brain. I've become part of this place instead of being a visitor. If the inside of me is as quiet as the world outside, then I share the most essential element with everything here. Being silent means being with nature in its reality, not the reality the narrator in my head creates.

I feel naked and vulnerable in the silence. Apparently the words in my head usually protect me by directing my attention and naming only certain parts of reality. In silence, the sounds and smells and movements hit my senses full on, with no buffer. My skin tingles and my internal organs feel as though they are dissolving before the onrush of energy and beauty. I am a speck in a huge silent shout of vitality.

"You live in silence; I live in silence," I say aloud. As soon as I speak, I'm different and separate again. I return to being silent.

I move beyond the maple, placing each foot carefully on fallen orange cedar fronds that crackle lightly. I hear a frog croak, a squirrel bark, and my pant legs rubbing together.

I'm listening with my ears and my eyes and my skin. The smells of wet mud and spicy pine hang in the air.

A small plane roars over the park, rattling the silence where I stand. The engine noise fades into the distance.

I realize I'm breathing with my mouth open so I can breathe soundlessly. It's hard to be silent for so long. It's like an isometric exercise: my habit of chattering in my head exerts a constant pressure against my intention to be quiet. When my intention weakens the slightest bit, my stronger habit wins and chatter begins again.

I lie in a single spot of sun and look up at a scruffy-looking maple. A leaf glows gold in the sun while up in the blue sky a wispy cloud blows by. I gaze at the spaces between the branches. It's easier to stay quiet inside when I focus between things. The air between things is more like silence itself—omnipresent, invisible, and nourishment for any sentence or branch that pushes through it.

Joining with nature in silence doesn't always feel peaceful. It can be surprisingly frightening to give up control and meet the world without the protection of words.

Usually, words protect me by directing my attention toward things that fit my world view, or by explaining the things that don't. Words comfort me or buffer the impact of anything my psyche might find upsetting. When I'm silent, anything can reach my attention.

Silence challenges me to meet nature without any internal disc jockey influencing my experience with explanations or warnings. I sense and react to exactly what is before me.

The next journal experience still amazes me. Simply being silent and attentive took me all the way from being over-loaded with a busyness mindset, through the settling-in process, into a joyous, wild communion. I was sitting at a beach park along Lake Washington, five minutes from my house. Even though the park is nearby, I usually have to push myself to get up and go. It's so easy to get complacent and just stay indoors. Once I'm there, I'm always glad.

Lake Washington   May

I woke up anxious. The house must be cleaned, the faucet repaired, the camper organized and packed, the propane leak checked, the battery recharged or replaced, my health insurance updated. The list goes on and on. At 6 A.M. the day is already impossible and I don't even want to begin.

I take my tea and cantaloupe to the porch. It's not raining and doesn't look as though it will, so I could go down to the beach after I eat. I haven't been there for days.

I'm only slightly torn between starting my chores and going to the beach. I can't imagine going through my whole day with this level of unhappiness. Maybe going to the water's edge can help.

I drive to the park, unload my beach chair, and wonder what I'll do when I get there. Should I let my angst speak? Should I try to praise the day?

I set up my chair. I feel both desperate and hopeless. I don't really believe that anything I do here can help me, so why not just do nothing?

I close my eyes and count my breaths, saying each number during the pause at the end of the exhale. I focus on that silent moment and pay attention to how my body feels. My muscles are tight; I ache with unhappiness.

I can stay focused on the silence and on what I'm feeling for only a few breaths before my mind wanders. I keep bringing my awareness back. I put no words on the feelings, I simply notice.

At breath number seventy-six, I'm able to hold the silence and really feel the ache. It pervades my whole body. I don't try to change it or put words to it. I just hold on to my goal of keeping silent at the end of each exhale.

At number one hundred, I open my eyes. I keep counting my breaths, starting over with number one. The sun has come blasting across the water while my eyes were closed, so I turn ninety degrees toward the shoreline and pull my sun visor across the side of my face to protect my eyes. I watch the water lap against a log on the sand. The log becomes my focus.

Within five breaths I'm crying. I have no words for it. I don't try to do anything with it. I simply count at the end of the exhale and focus on silence and whatever I'm feeling.

I cry and sniffle for one hundred counts. The unhappiness leaks out slowly while the beauty of the rippling water around the log seeps in. I close my eyes for another hundred counts.

With my eyes closed, the world of smells and sounds and feelings comes alive. Tears continue to leak out from between my eyelashes. I still don't understand what's happening, but I hold on to the numbers and the bubble of silence at the end of the exhale like a woman overboard holds on to a life preserver.

When I'm busy with the tasks of my life, I wonder why I bother to meditate. Now the meditator in me says, *I have the right to be here.*

I find myself taking a deep breath. The silent part of me, the meditator, is stretching out inside my body and then beyond my body, expanding into the still air over the lake. This silent one can't complete my list of tasks, but she has the right to some time, just like the playful part of me has the right to some time.

72

I savor the sweet scent of a spring morning after a night of rain. Now, as I stretch out into the silence, this moment is a gentle hand soothing me. Birdcalls are small blips in the silence. Even my sniffles are only blips in the silence.

I keep counting. I open my eyes again and the beauty of the log at my feet is stunning. My world consists of numbered breaths, a gentle silence, and waves of tears that come and go.

As my sniffles subside, I feel my silence resting gently on top of the water. Something inside slows down. As I slow, I become one with the day. It's as though I'd been a gear spinning too fast to connect with the gear beside me. Finally I hit the same speed and the same quietness as the day so I can mesh with it.

It's an exquisite day. Fat gray clouds cover the sun most of the time; moist air pushes softly against my face. Birds and lapping water sing on a magical silent stage. The silence between the sounds is as precious as the sounds themselves. I drink up the smell of green grass and sweet apple blossoms.

After ten minutes, my silence still hangs over the lake. I have the right to be here. I have the right to be silent and savor a silent experience of the day.

My undefined angst is gone. I've done nothing but pay attention to it in silence. When the waves from the wake of a boat hit shore, the music sends thrills through my body.

Despite the effort it may take to keep a silent mind, and despite the discomfort it may cause to let go of control, the joining that happens in silence can feel like being at home.

In *Women Who Run with the Wolves,* Clarissa Pinkola Estes writes about the woman who needs nature and silence:

> *For this woman, the inlet to her deep home is evoked by silence. . . . For her, the sound of wind through a great loom of trees is silence. For her, the crash of a mountain stream is silence. For her, thunder is silence. For her, the natural order of nature, which asks nothing in return, is her life-giving silence.*

Unfortunately, silence is hard to come by. It's so much easier to commune deeply with the silence of nature when the environment around us is free of civilized noises, but even at Banff National Park, in the first journal entry, I had to contend with traffic sounds. A man who records nature sounds for musicians told me he can rarely record fifteen minutes of untainted sounds in wilderness areas because airplanes fly everywhere.

I wonder what the world would be like if we truly valued

silence. I like to imagine that someday I'll visit a new town and the tourist map will be sprinkled with green Q's: spots local residents have set aside as Quiet Zones for communing. Maybe nature maps will also be sprinkled with green Q's, so when I visit a beach I will know that people at the Q beaches value silence and privacy.

It's a lovely fantasy, but, for now, we can't count on finding silence, so we have to create our own silence inside. One of the quickest ways to reach inner silence is to pay attention to your senses. Walk barefoot or crawl in the grass. Touch, smell, squeeze, or press your cheek against anything you encounter. Don't let your mind comment, just enjoy the sensual experience. After five minutes with only silence and your senses, you will be refreshed and alert. Try it on a coffee break!

Like relaxing, being silent gets easier the more you practice it. If being silent with nature is not yet in your repertoire, you're about to add a gem to your life.

Tips for Using Silence

1. Count your breaths and sink into the stillness at the end of the exhale.
2. Count your breaths and alternate opening and closing your eyes every ten breaths.
3. Pay attention to the silence and the silent objects around you.

4. *Decide* to be silent.
5. Listen.
6. Pay attention to how your body feels.
7. Breathe and move quietly, move slowly.
8. Notice the spaces between things.
9. Use thought-stopping, or gently say "thought" when you notice a thought, and then bring your attention back to being silent.
10. Imagine you are the meditator part of yourself or some other part that enjoys silence.
11. Pay attention to your senses.

In this chapter, you will learn to take charge of your internal dialogue so you can use the words in your mind to deepen your communing experience. Talking to yourself and talking aloud to nature are two ways to get focused and stay focused. You can consciously choose words that will put you in a particular frame of mind, or you can attend to and learn from the words that spontaneously emerge.

5
USING WORDS

Even though I love to use silence for communing with nature, many times I can't start with silence. My mind is too busy, and only by talking to myself in a louder voice can I override the chatter inside my head.

In the first chapter, I mentioned a few ways I use words to pack up my busyness mindset: I list what I'm leaving behind and I state what I'm looking forward to during my visit with nature. When that's not enough, I keep talking to myself. I'm hoping my mind won't be able to hold two conversations at once— I'm hoping my busyness voice will give up.

The easiest way to shut out my preoccupations is to describe the scene around me. When I say what I see and feel and hear, I automatically have to pay more attention to my surroundings.

Sometimes as I'm describing my surroundings, a particular phrase sends a tingle through my body. Repeating that phrase will help keep me focused.

Repeating words also creates a pattern in my memory. At some point later in the day, I can say that phrase again and recreate the feeling or remember the lesson from my time communing. Words are a wonderful form of luggage; they encapsulate an experience so we can take it with us wherever we go.

In the following experience I was at Beachwood, the little cottage only two hours from my Seattle home that I go to whenever I can. While it gets its share of airplane and boat noises, it's still a peaceful retreat from the city.

Beachwood   January

Sitting on the porch over the bay, I watch clouds drift by and gulls swoop. Music drifts out to me from the cottage. It's exquisitely serene. The music could be the background for a movie: *A woman sits, contentedly basking in the beauty of the scene before her.*

Somehow, in my life, it's never so easy to reach or

hold that contented feeling. Instead, I find myself thinking about my To-Do list. It's frustrating to be dragged away from this peaceful loveliness by worries. Right now I don't want to think about anything, plan anything, or worry about anything.

I focus on the gulls. They seem completely carefree. They are so high above the water that I can't imagine they are looking for food; my fantasy is that they're soaring simply for pleasure. As a matter of fact, in my time at this cottage I've seen the gulls do very little work. They float or they soar. Occasionally I see them "at work" dropping a clam to the beach to crack. Cormorants also seem to spend their time enjoying themselves. Certainly, they dive for food from time to time, but I often see them just hanging out on that pier.

The sun peeks through and kisses my face. I let my consciousness stretch out into the ease of the floating clouds. Why can't my life be like the gulls' lives? Why can't my life be mostly pleasure, mostly soaring? Am I addicted to struggle? Is our whole culture addicted to it? I don't want to be. I don't believe my way to the life force is through struggle. I believe I meet the life force most easily in its natural state, which is, most of the time, beauty and slowness.

Thoughts about the work week ahead start

grabbing my attention. What can I say about the day right this moment to keep me anchored in the present?

"I see your tiny waves sparkle and your fat clouds sail. I love the blue sky that beckons me to relax. Your breeze pats my face and rattles the alder trees behind me. This is heaven right now."

At those words, a wave of relaxation washes through me, and I immediately come back into my body. I feel the warmth of the sun, I hear the leaves rustling, I smell the salty air.

"This is heaven right now," I say to myself anytime a future thought enters my head. Yes, this is heaven, and the only way to enjoy it is to pay attention to it, even if I have to narrate to myself to take up the internal airwaves and force out other thinking.

Throughout the day I hold the thought that I have the right to a life that's mostly enjoyable. "This is heaven right now," I say to myself over and over. I listen to music on the drive home and look at the trees that pass, ignoring the buildings and signs. When I focus on what's heavenly, I can always find something nice to notice, even if it's simply that I'm warm and dry while a sudden rainstorm pounds on my windshield.

I consciously push away worries that want

attention. "Not now," I tell them. "Now I get to be in heaven." I hum while unpacking the car and I think often of the soaring gulls. "This is heaven right now."

Describing my surroundings took me out of my analytical frame of mind and put me into my senses. Narrating made me pay attention to the natural world I wanted to commune with, instead of paying attention to the stories in my imagination.

You may have noticed that I begin most of my journal entries with a description of my environment. This isn't just a literary device. I write down what's around me to make myself pay closer attention, to help myself *see*.

Annie Dillard writes about two kinds of seeing. One kind of seeing "involves a letting go. When I see this way I sway transfixed and emptied." The other kind of seeing requires words:

> *Seeing is of course very much a matter of verbalization. Unless I call my attention to what passes before my eyes, I simply won't see it. . . . I have to say the words, describe what I'm seeing. If Tinker Mountain erupted, I'd be likely to notice. But if I want to notice the lesser cataclysms of valley life, I have to maintain in my head a running description of the present.*

At Beachwood, once I was paying close attention to my environment, I had a reaction, and I put that reaction into words: "This is heaven right now." That phrase then encapsulated the experience for me so that whenever I repeated it, it functioned like a time machine, taking me back to the same state of observant, appreciative openness I had experienced earlier.

Words are so powerful. How we talk to ourselves can literally determine what we notice and how we feel. As a therapist, I often ask my clients to pay attention to how they talk to themselves. Once they are aware of their internal dialogue, they can decide to talk to themselves differently.

Sometimes I consciously choose the words I want to say. More frequently, words emerge on their own as my unconscious responds both to my inner needs and to the scene before me.

In the following experience, I slowed my words, and it was the pace as much as the words themselves that brought me joy. It was as though the brief silence between words lets each one settle in more deeply than usual. The words became like a haiku poem, penetrating and illuminating the essence of the moment.

The experience takes place in a "mini-park" three blocks from my office where I often take my lunch. An elderly couple sold their hillside home to the city, and neighbors put the wooded sections of their lots into a modified land trust whereby they get tax breaks for agreeing not to develop the land. Once the city removed the house, voila!—we have a mini-park with woods, a yard, and a view.

Mini-park   October

I have a little time to relax before I go back to work. I close my eyes and breathe in the sweet smells of clover and freshly cut grass. The wind rattles the maples and madrones over my head, then abruptly stops. I drop like a stone into a sudden silence.

I count my breaths, saying the number of each breath at the still moment after the exhale. Then I let the numbers fade, and haiku-like words fill their places.

Sun streaks . . . (inhale/exhale) . . . rib cage bones . . .
(inhale/exhale) . . . casting shadows . . .
(inhale/exhale) . . . like venetian blinds. . . .
Soft air presses . . . cheek hairs . . . flattening them . . .
just a little. . . .
I am you . . . day . . . I am you. . . .
And the essence . . . of this . . . is not air . . . or sun
warmth. . . .
The essence . . . is willingness. . . .

> *My heart . . . is a bowl . . . of willingness. . . .*
> *Willing . . . to be you.*

Tears fill my eyes and a flash of pleasure ripples through me, as though all the cells in its path are bursting open to make room for the beauty of the day.

The words that came to me in the park do not make a great poem. But they caught my experience and slowed it down so I could savor it. They helped me be in the moment.

I'd like you to experience the power of slowing words right now. Read the poem in the previous journal entry again and match each set of words to only one breath. It will take about two minutes.

Was it difficult to read those words slowly? Our busyness mindsets are usually working at a pace that makes it hard to commune. Slowing your words can calm your mind.

Do you feel more relaxed and centered after reading the poem slowly? I'm always surprised how much a simple two-minute exercise can relax me.

So far I've been using words to keep myself focused on my surroundings or on my goals. I've mainly been talking to myself. One day in the arboretum, I used words to talk to nature, and in the process I entered a different kind of communing experience. While it may seem silly to talk to something in nature, I've had some of my most powerful and surprising communing experiences by doing exactly that. I encourage you to try it!

Washington Park Arboretum   November

It's 8 A.M. and I'm standing beneath the almost-nude limbs of a Japanese maple. At my feet, the ground is carpeted with brilliant rain-slicked red leaves. I repeat a phrase I made up years ago when I wanted help staying focused in nature: "Life force, power clear, beauty, touch me."

At the word *beauty,* the vibrant energy of the red leaves at my feet flies up and through me. I'm not used to life-force energy coming up through my feet. It's quite an amazing feeling.

It fades until I repeat the phrase again and come to the word beauty. Yes, there's the rush. *Beauty* is the key that opens the door in me so I can receive what's right here all the time. I want the life force's power and beauty to touch me— today its power is in its red color, and the magic word is beauty.

I'm intrigued that the word beauty so consistently accesses this rush of connection. I know there is great power in naming. Is that it? Does correctly naming what's before me open me to its essence? Does naming open a level of understanding that's deeper, or create a framework that brings it to life— like touching a flame to a candle?

One could contemplate an unlit candle from many angles, touch it with many things, but the flame brings out its true essence. Could a word be like that? Is that the power of poetry, of chanting, of writing?

Everywhere I stroll I say, "Hello, beauty," or "You're magnificent, beauty." Each time there is a rush of recognition and delight.

I walk on a carpet of gold witch hazel leaves, breathing in the sweet scent of the tree's strange spidery flowers. I put my face into a branch full of red maple leaves and kiss one. I study an intricately curled brown leaf hanging limply on a peach maple tree.

I walk into the arms of my favorite bright yellow tree. "Hello, beauty. I know you're fleeting in my life. I know as a human animal with limited capacities I can't hold you, but thank you for being here today."

I didn't decide in advance to use the word *beauty* as a focus word, but when saying it gave me that rush of delight, I paid attention. Speaking to nature can have a winnowing effect like that. When I say what I see or what I feel or what I want, at some point in my monologue, the wordy chaff blows away and the essential grains of truth are revealed clean and clear.

Talking aloud has an added benefit. When I talk out loud, I can follow one train of thought to its end. Ordinarily, different points of view constantly interrupt each other inside my brain, and I flit from one perspective to another. When I talk aloud, only one internal voice can speak at a time, and I can get more deeply into its particular viewpoint and wisdom.

When I talk aloud, I also give myself a subtle but powerful message that I'm worth listening to—that my life is worth examining and taking seriously.

Tips for Using Words

1. Use words to outshout your busy mind. Talk louder than your habitual chatter by describing the scene around you or stating your intentions. Your busy mind will give up.
2. Use words to focus your attention. As you describe your surroundings, you'll become more aware of them. You force yourself to be in the present moment when you name either what you see, what you feel, or what you need.

3. Use words to discover what you're feeling or what you need. Try different words and see which one you react to.

4. Use words to communicate with yourself——either to give yourself a pep talk or to correct some bad thinking patterns. Words are part of your relationship with yourself.

5. Repeat and contemplate the words that seem to spring into your head. Maybe they are words from a life force or great consciousness; maybe they are from your own wise self inside.

6. Slowly say haiku-like words to take you deeper into an experience. Match the words to your exhales.

7. Use words to solidify your learning If your experience is confusing, words will force you to clarify it. Once you can put an experience into words, that experience is easier to remember and integrate into the rest of your life.

8. Use words to express yourself and to build a new kind of relationship with nature. After you talk to a tree, it will seem less alien.

In this chapter, you will move from the general use of words to a specific use of words. You will learn how to use mantras. Mantras can be used to settle in or to create a communing experience. A mantra is a syllable, a word, or a series of words you repeat in order to focus and clear your mind. Syllables without meaning can simply relax you and make you receptive; words with meaning can determine what you pay attention to.

6
USING MANTRAS

I learned my first mantra in a college yoga class from a white-haired German man named Yogi Haeckel. He was seventy-five years old, spoke broken English, and ate a lot of vegetarian pizza. Aside from a few idiosyncratic memories like these, I don't remember much from that course. I do, however, remember the syllables of the mantra he taught the class: *Satnam siriwah padme guruji* (pronounced *saht*-nahm *see*-ree-wha *pahd*-may *goo*-roo-jee). The rhythm is the same as: I like butterscotch, I like butterscotch.

Over the years, I've used this mantra to relax, to meditate, or to settle in for communing. The simple sounds of the chant block out the words of my chattering thoughts, the rhythm is as soothing as any lullaby, and the discipline of focusing on one thing calms my flitting mind. I don't remember the meaning of the words and I don't want to. Part of the reason it has been so helpful is that it doesn't make me think about anything—it helps me stop thinking.

Some meditation schools say that the meaning of the mantra is all-important. Other schools say that the tone and quality of the sound is most important. Lawrence LeShan, Ph.D., author of *How to Meditate*, suggests you can even choose two names at random in a phone book and combine the first syllable of each name to create a mantra. "The main determination [in choosing a mantra] is that it should be something that feels comfortable," says Swami Ramananda of the Integral Yoga Institute in New York City.

Some people sing their mantras, like the Gregorian chants of the Catholic church or the Hare Krishna chants. Some people say their mantras aloud in a monotone. As Diane Ackerman writes in *A Natural History of the Senses,* "Chant 'om,' or any other mantra, in a solid, prolonged tone, and you will feel the bones in your head, as well as the cartilage in your sternum, vibrate. It's like a massage from the inside, very soothing." I usually don't say my mantra aloud but repeat it only in my mind. That way I can still be aware of the sounds and the silence around me. If I want to block out noises, I say it aloud.

In the following experience, using my Satnam mantra helped me relax, be present, and feel connected to life.

Beachwood   February

What a surprise it was to wake up to a blue sky! It's been raining for days.

This morning, however, I sit on the bulkhead above the incoming tide and watch the sun rise over a bank of clouds to the east. Sparkles reflect up from the water into the wispy clouds overhead to become rainbows. Suddenly the plain round pebbles and the braided channels of runoff water on the beach are glistening beauties.

I've come here greedy and hungry—reaching for every sensation. I've forgotten the difference between reaching for nature and connecting with nature. The rational part of me that's generally in charge has such a hard time acknowledging that it cannot connect me to nature all by itself. It must give over its power to the quiet, receptive, meditative parts of me.

I close my eyes and relax. I feel the sun on my face and see its orange light behind my eyelids. The melody of the waves seems to become louder, though I know it's merely because my listening has changed.

I breathe slowly. I count from five to zero and tell myself to relax a little more with each number. I let go of any tension as completely as I can when I reach zero. When my brain starts to chatter, I count from five to zero again. And again.

Once my body is relaxed, I stop counting and silently chant my old familiar mantra: *Satnam siriwah padme guruji.* The syllables soothe me and slow my thoughts so I can be present.

I go to that deeply relaxed, deeply still place inside and a quiet smile spreads through my body. Yes, I like to be here. With each Satnam, I feel as though I'm taking a step deeper inside myself and a step closer to the life force.

A friend suggested I try imagining that my awareness is seated in my old reptilian brain, deep in the back and bottom of my skull. When I feel myself going deeper, I wonder if I'm going deeper into that brain. Am I getting closer to how animals feel in their lives?

I move closer and closer to the life force, slowly, until I face it and touch it. I keep chanting. I feel as though I am leaning into a soft balloon as tall as the sky. The front of my body sinks into this lifeforce balloon and is held and comforted. I don't dissolve into it, it doesn't surround me. It's more like the feeling I get when I lean up against a giant old tree trunk and let its energy into me.

There is no message, no revelation. There is only an experience: the touch of the life force, the sparkles of the sun, the song of the tide. When I can manage to be deeply quiet and present, I discover delight.

I used my mantra on this day to quiet my mind; any thoughts that wanted to interrupt me had to push through the words of the chant. I also used it to help me stay focused on what I was experiencing.

When unusual perceptions arise—like the sensation of leaning into the life force—a mantra provides a constant touchstone of something that's familiar. In some subtle way, it reassures me so I can simply experience whatever is happening without running from it, changing it, or explaining it. A friend who travels frequently for his work mentioned the stabilizing effect of his mantra: "I meditate every morning using my mantra so that no matter what city I wake up in, I always feel at home. Not only am I doing something familiar, chanting takes me to the peaceful place inside myself that's constant and 'home.'"

Sometimes I consciously use the pace of the chant to slow me down. I'll start chanting rapidly, especially if I have a lot of thoughts running around in my brain; then, bit by bit, I chant more slowly. As the chant slows, my breathing slows, my body relaxes, and I can be present.

Usually I chant just until I relax and slow down. Occasionally, however, I play with the mantra long after I'm relaxed, slowing down the pace even more or imagining the syllables floating through the air.

One of the most powerful communing experiences I've ever had occurred when I simply stilled my mind, set a boundary, and chanted. It happened a few years after I began communing regularly and it took me by complete surprise. It was as though, in Annie Dillard's words, "I had been my whole life a bell, and never knew it until at that moment I was lifted and struck."

Washington Park Arboretum   April

I sit in a nook of untended bushes and grass. While I eat my granola, I shift my position ever so slightly to make the dewdrops on the grass shine with rainbow colors. Then I decide to commune.

First I count my breaths to one hundred with my eyes closed, just stilling my mind and being aware of the sounds and the feel of the sun and breeze. It's a noisy day, full of traffic rumbles, siren shrieks, and a buzzing chain saw.

I imagine a boundary dome of white light around me and the little meadow surrounding me, so all those noises are "out there" and can be as loud and discordant as they want. In here with me is just my peaceful meadow with its birdsongs and silence.

As soon as my boundary is in place, I feel delighted and calm. This little meadow can nourish me with its beauty and I can nourish it with my love.

Yes, I can have this. I don't have to worry about the outside noises, the outside world. I can be in this world, just this size, and love it without feeling responsible for anything outside. Most of what's outside I can't change anyway.

After the one hundred breaths I start to chant silently: *Satnam siriwah padme guruji.* As soon as I begin the chant, I get goosebumps all over and a tingling inside. Suddenly tears are falling and I'm sobbing and I don't have any words for why.

Am I crying because the love and delight have welled up inside me so strongly they have to burst out in tears? Is my heart aching because it feels so good to be home, to feel home all the way through me, in this little grassy nook?

For twenty years, on and off, I've used this chant, but never before have I had this experience. With each syllable of Satnam, I feel myself inside the sound of the chant, inside the life of the meadow, and inside the power of the life force all at the same time.

The bushes, the grass, the air all sparkle with a

clarity and a luminosity I've never seen before; and at the same time I feel luminous, too. It's as though centuries of dust have been instantly wiped from the planet and from my psyche and heart, so we all shine and receive each other clearly. The blast of that direct connection has ripped me open and filled me with energy.

Somehow, stilling myself, putting a boundary around this small parcel of earth, and pouring all my love into it has made it more real than any of a thousand times I've loved nature. "I can love you," I say to the meadow. "You're just my size. You're not huge or spectacular. You're common grass and a motley assortment of bushes and trees, just as I'm a motley assortment of human characteristics. And right now, you're mine. You're mine to love, mine to share this moment with. Together, we know life is a miracle. Together, we are the miracle."

I start slowing down the Satnam chant, drawing out each syllable, reveling in the peace of each one, not wanting it to end. Then words come from a voice inside—*with faith the size of a mustard seed*—and I sob again.

Yes, that's what I have: just a tiny bit of faith. I have no idea why I'm having this amazing experience of love and joy. I certainly haven't earned it in any way, through goodness or spiritual practices. It's sheer gift.

It came because I have faith, even as tiny as a mustard seed, that brought me here and made me be still without having any idea what I might find.

I feel so grateful for that faith, as though I've discovered a pearl within myself I hadn't realized was there. It's a pearl I've been building speck by speck: coming to the arboretum, walking, looking, loving nature, going to mountains and creeks, always trying to open a little more to being present, to being touched. So many times my rational mind has not been at all in agreement: *Oh, you were there yesterday,* it says. Or, *It's just a little park, it won't be anything special.* But the buried spark of faith always drives me and dumps me, unaware and grumbling, into the middle of nature to be healed again, to put another speck into my faith pearl.

I never know what will happen when I commune. That's part of the adventure and the risk. Sometimes nothing happens but boredom. I'm too tired or too tense; my hormones are off or some other mysterious body chemistry interferes with my best intentions. But sometimes, again in Annie Dillard's words, "You wait in all naturalness without expectation or hope, emptied, translucent, and that which comes rocks and topples you; it will shear, loose, launch, winnow, grind."

It's worth trying to connect deeply with nature again and again because connecting gets easier and the "mustard seed" grows. Because connecting feeds you in a way nothing else can. Obviously you don't have to spend weeks or go to spectacular wilderness to be touched deeply. If you have already etched your connection with nature into your cells, a noisy park and an hour can be enough.

I should warn you that you most likely will never have the same experience twice. After this amazing experience in the arboretum, I was ready for it to happen again. Worse than that, I was perched and waiting for it. My self-consciousness eliminated any possibility of being open enough to receive much of anything for months.

On that day in the arboretum, however, relaxing and creating a boundary set the stage. Chanting my mantra gave me the calm openness that allowed the experience to happen, and chanting provided a stability that let me stay open.

Sometimes I repeat my mantra until it feels right to stop. Other times, my busy mind is too agitated to accept an open-ended chanting period. My mind persistently wanders until I set a limit on the time I'll spend chanting. Maybe it wants to be certain I won't get lost in a mantra-induced altered state. Maybe it can only agree to let go of control for a certain amount of time. In any case, there are days when I need to decide in advance that I'll chant Satnam only ten times or only ten minutes, for instance. As the final chants approach, I feel an added alertness, an extra effort to pay attention and not let daydreams take over. It's as though an internal coach prompts, *Listen up, now. I have only two repetitions left. Better get down to business.*

I can see the benefit of using the same chant for a long time. After twenty years of using this mantra off and on, I have quite a relationship with it. As soon as I say the first few syllables, my body knows that it's time to relax and my mind knows it will soon have to stop chattering. Unless I'm particularly distracted, my unconscious associations and memories pull me pretty quickly into a meditative state.

Mantras come in many shapes and sizes. I have my regular mantra, but I also experiment with others to see what they can add to my experience in nature.

Yoho National Park, British Columbia, Canada   June

I sit in my beach chair on the shore of Lake O'Hara. The day is chilly and gorgeous—three-quarters clouds, one-quarter blue sky.

I'm being lazy today. There will be no steep climbs or strenuous paddling for me. I want to simply saunter around Lake O'Hara and set up my beach chair as the mood strikes.

In the lake below me, a dozen jagged rocks pierce the perfect reflection of a glacier-draped mountain, while overhead, towering peaks pierce a huge sky. To each side of me, piles of square stones are carpeted with moss and decorated with bonsai fir trees.

A breeze shatters the reflection in the water and swirls around my lips, first so lightly I can barely feel it, then with recognizable gusts. Pushing, pushing against my lips and cheeks, it carries spicy whiffs of pine.

I close my eyes and count my breaths. There are not many thoughts to stop today. Long before I reach seventy, I've settled into the silence between the numbers.

I chant *Satnam siriwah padme guruji,* mostly with my eyes closed. I can feel the bigness of the silence and of the mountains better with my eyes closed. I alternate between silence and chanting Satnam.

My mind wants to meditate, but my stomach wants to eat. I move to a viewpoint near a falls to eat lunch, then settle down to commune again.

I remember something I read in *Meetings with Remarkable Women: Buddhist Teachers in America.* One Buddhist teacher said she had been told she could skip the hundreds of koans (teaching riddles) if she just meditated on the mantra *Mu* and understood it. A student said she felt Mu was dark and a little scary.

Silently and slowly, I chant, *Mu.* I don't know if

reading about the student's fear has triggered my reaction, but Mu is very uncomfortable for me to chant right now. My throat constricts into a pain like tonsillitis. My eyes begin to tear. I feel heavy and stuck in mud. A black tunnel goes down my trunk to my tailbone. Mu seems to be the underbelly of life: suffering, death, slime. I try to make it lighter—I try to imagine a flower blossoming as I chant. It still feels heavy. I open my eyes to gaze at the lake and glaciered mountain as I chant, only to find my eyes drawn to the dead branches under the water. I imagine the mountains built on a million deaths.

I switch to the chant *Om.* Yesterday I read in *The Joys of Meditation* that only recluses and renunciates should use Om. I obviously don't qualify, but I want to get away from Mu. Om feels expansive, as though it holds all the myriad bits of the universe with plenty of space to spare.

I then switch to my old mantra, Satnam. It feels light and nourishing, like a warm breeze moving across the lake.

Finally, I choose an English word to chant: *Soften.* Of all the chants, Soften touches me most deeply. My heart opens and tears of joy spring to my eyes. The lake, the mountains, and the sky all pour into my open chest. It's overwhelming and sweet.

What a lovely word soften is. It says, *Don't reach,*

or think, or strive—don't even be. Turn into a cloud.
Let this life in deeply. Let it seep into pores and cells,
let it swirl around muscles. Let it permeate your soul.
Trust it like a friend. Live with it in you gently,
openly. Don't understand life. Just live with it.

When I say soften, I almost feel as though I could
let all of life slide into me and out again like a
breeze. Now the tears feel like relief, not like the
constriction of the tears I shed with Mu. My belly
fills out into deep breaths.

Clear ripples send waves of sensuous relaxation
through me like a massage. *Soften*, I chant. *Soften.*
The liquid light enters my chest.

Sometimes I seem to become immune to the word
soften, so I say it only every four breaths instead of
each breath. I let there be silence in between.

I close my eyes and say, *What is softer?* The muscles in my shoulders relax. Silence. *Soften.* . . .
Silence. *Soften.* . . . Silence. *What is softer?* I find
myself noticing everything that's soft. Ripples are
soft. The air is soft. Light rising up a slope of gray
rock behind a cloud shadow is soft. I'm soft.

Often I chant a mantra when I begin communing. It clears
and slows my mind, blocks out inner chatter, and helps me
be receptive.

When I chanted Soften, however, I became active. I gave myself an instruction to follow. Instead of being open to whatever happened, I focused on softness. I didn't want to feel just anything, I wanted to feel softer. I didn't want to notice just anything, I wanted to notice things related to softness. Repeating the word soften took me deeper and deeper—not into the abstract meaning of softness—but into the experience of softness.

Because soften is an English word, it may not seem like a mantra. Most people expect mantras to be in a foreign or an ancient language. And yet, every mantra is made from words that are, or have been, someone's native tongue. As long as I'm experimenting, I can try some English mantras to see what they are like. Some people meditate on words such as *peace, God,* or *one.*

Trager Mentastics, which is a form of meditation-in-motion, suggests three English phrases to repeat as you move slowly: "What is lighter? What is softer? What is freer?" Repeating these phrases brings you into a state of "hook-up," or a "blending and becoming one with the energy force that surrounds all living things." Again, the three phrases direct your attention and help you stay focused.

Directive mantras are particularly helpful in noisy or ugly parts of town. You can screen out certain sounds or sights by focusing in on your mantra.

A directive mantra can also put short, rejuvenating nature connections into your day. Choose a mantra in the morning as you eat breakfast on the stoop. Then use it during breaks in your day: go outside to commune or stay inside and remember the feeling of communing.

A client of mine said she lost her connection with nature when she stopped smoking. Previously, she had gone outdoors to smoke several times a day, but now she had "no excuse" to go outside. I suggested she take a directive mantra outside instead of a cigarette.

Feel free to experiment with mantras of your own. Try using English words, non-English words, and sounds. Each kind of mantra will affect your experience in nature differently.

Tips for Using a Mantra

1. Silently repeat a sound, a word, or a phrase rhythmically.
2. You can use words from any language.
3. Your goal is to focus *all* your awareness on the mantra. When other thoughts interrupt, simply return to repeating the mantra.
4. You can match your repetitions to the rhythm of your breathing, or you can use a completely different rhythm. Sometimes it helps calm the mind and body to start the repetitions at a conversational speed and then slow them down.
5. You can repeat the mantra with your eyes open, with

your eyes closed, or with your eyes alternating between open and closed.

6. You can set a time period to chant, or you can set a goal of a certain number of repetitions to do, or you can leave it open-ended. Sometimes having a limit on time or repetitions will give you added impetus to focus well in the time you have.

In this chapter, you will add another technique to your communing repertoire and move toward a more personal relationship with nature. While silence and slow motion helped you merge with nature, getting close turns that merging into a feeling of kinship.

7
GETTING CLOSE

Getting close to something natural is a great way to settle in and begin communing. It relaxes you because it limits your choices and the stimuli hitting your senses.

Several years ago I had a long wait at the Los Angeles airport, so I wandered outside to see what I might find that could reconnect me with nature. It had been a hectic, concrete-and-traffic-filled day, and the prospect of sitting in yet another cement building didn't appeal to me.

I strolled along the sidewalk until a young tree by the baggage claim caught my eye. I picked my way through the shrubbery, leaned against the tree's trunk, and stroked its corklike bark. Immediately the noise and chaos of the airport faded as I focused on the bark's intricate patterns and textures. I could feel the beauty and aliveness of the tree soothing and refreshing me. The tree was a solid and simple resting spot in my complicated day. Fifteen minutes later when I went back inside, I felt calm and refreshed.

You might think you'll only need to use getting close in town, where noise and distractions sometimes make communing difficult. In the following journal entry, however, I needed to use getting close on a beautiful state park beach.

May

Larrabee State Park, near Bellingham, Washington

I sit twelve feet from the incoming tide behind a line of green seaweed that is being pushed with each wave. At 5 P.M., this is not a quiet spot.

I had expected the beach to be empty. The tide's nearly in, so there are no tide pools to explore, and usually people go back to their camps about now for dinner. I was wrong. Three wailing children just trudged to the top of the bank, but as soon as they got out of earshot, two shouting teenage girls descended. They are laughing about crooked wedding veils. I am trying to hear the sound of the tide.

Maybe if I focus on the things I love I won't notice the noise so much. A bird chirps overhead, waves slosh in, and sun bakes the back of my writing hand. The San Juan Islands are blue lumps across the sparkling water. Airplane motors fill the air. It is hard to stay focused on the beauty when I am spending so much energy trying to block out civilized noises and sore teeth from dental work yesterday.

I go to the very edge of the beach and climb onto smooth rocks sculpted by wind and water. Here water slides and bonks while it sculpts, playing all the tones of a xylophone. With my back to the people, I can be alone in my self-made cove. My body is one bank of the cove, the sinuous rock wall the other.

Children shout nearby and clomp among the rocks. Even turning my back on them and writing down the beauty around me can't keep them from intruding on my peace. I move closer to the water until I am sitting only three inches from a pool in a rock basin.

Golden ripples stroke a strip of rounded pink rock lying underwater. Every pebble around it is magnified. An army of tiny black snails perch on the rock's mounds. *Gentle colors, gentle swirls, can you seduce me away from the distractions?*

It seems unfair that the loud and the obnoxious dominate the world. The loudest person on the beach determines its mood. The most obnoxious event of the day will intrude on my thoughts. I bring the peaceful into my life by an act of will—by consciously focusing *here,* by getting so close that my whole visual range is filled with only beauty, by putting a mental boundary around this little ten-foot circle and calling it mine. I let the silences and the sounds here be mine, I make the sounds outside be other.

I can block out the people and noises somewhat, but I want to be more deeply connected. I want to commune here.

I lie down and put my face six inches from the water so I can watch the tiny black snails wriggle up the rock. When I place my fingertips in the shallow-est water, I'm pulled into every wavelet by the shock of cold. I arch my hand over a strand of bright green eel grass while it writhes in the water, feeling the tiny tremors in my fingertips as it scrapes against the sandstone floor. As long as I'm absorbed in the sensations of this world and the questions of this world (Is that pile of snails fighting or copulat-ing?), the shouting world is farther away. As long as my heart embraces this world completely, I can commune without being distracted.

When I leave the beach an hour later, I feel as though I have wrested a gem of peace and beauty from the heap of noise and distractions at the beach. I am tired, but I am smiling a pink smile full of golden ripples and little black snails.

When I get close to something natural, I am immersing my eyes and my mind in it, and usually it is quite beautiful. Just a short vacation in total beauty is immensely refreshing.

Getting close to something in nature is so simple, yet so profound. When I focus on one thing, I leave the big, overwhelming world behind. My world is just this little bit of nature right in front of me, and it's small enough for me to relate to.

Getting close automatically limits me to one choice. It makes me less scattered and more grounded. I'm not jumping from phone call to phone call, or from vista to vista. I can experience this one bit of life completely. Kabat-Zinn calls this decision to limit oneself "voluntary simplicity":

> *Voluntary simplicity means going fewer places in one day rather than more, seeing less so I can see more, doing less so I can do more, acquiring less so I can have more.*

While getting close was a survival strategy at the beach at Larrabee, getting close and voluntary simplicity often have to be conscious decisions. In a world overflowing with delectable choices, deciding to limit my options can take some discipline and determination.

The next experience takes place at a cabin in Oregon. Although the cabin is small and rustic and has no indoor plumbing, it's a perfect retreat in shady woods.

Mount Hood National Forest, Oregon   August

This afternoon I get to sit for a while above the creek in front of the cabin and just be. I'm too sore and wiped out from roofing to do anything else. I look down at the rushing water and I know that to be really touched by it, I have to go down close to it.

The view is peaceful and lovely from up here. I can see trees and rocks and water. But nothing catches my attention. The song of the creek is just a roar. I can't hear any of the individual melodies the water is playing on particular rocks and logs.

I can sit up here and know that each little rock has its own whirlpool, water sheet, or trickle that changes ever so slightly from moment to moment, but I can't feel it. From here, the creek is a single moving mass. If I were to sit two feet away instead, I would experience an infinite variety of splashes and caresses; I would see water rippling over pebbles or dancing up against boulders. Its changes and multiple facets would resonate with my own.

Down there is one little niche that mimics my current state of mind, and other niches that demonstrate other ways of being: calmer, wilder. Up close, the creek would both match my mind and offer it new possibilities.

The closer I am to anything in life, the more

completely I'm drawn in—both to its unique reality and to its mirroring of my reality. Well, I've talked myself into it. I'm going down to the creek.

When I go to nature, I'm often drawn to the sweeping vista: the Grand Canyon, the plunging waterfall, or the calving glacier. These are the points of interest on maps and the destinations around which I plan my vacations. And yet, it's difficult to make an intimate connection with a vista.

Many times, after I've been overwhelmed and numbed by a grand view, I settle down to sit with something small and close—a flower reaching over the rim of the canyon, a rock being misted by the waterfall, a slowly crawling insect. Focusing on the details of this small object or being opens me up to a more personal connection to nature.

The prince in *The Little Prince* is devoted to one rose. He teaches the narrator that when you value an individual flower, you find love:

> *"The men where you live," said the little prince, "raise five thousand roses in the same garden— and they do not find in it what they are looking for."*
>
> *"They do not find it," I replied.*
>
> *"And yet what they are looking for could be found in one single rose. . . ."*

Walt Whitman puts it another way: "And there is no object so soft but it makes a hub for the wheeled universe." When you get close to a leaf, that leaf becomes the hub of your universe. You may find a rush of respect akin to joy washing through you. By your actions you are saying, *Even though I am surrounded by a forest full of leaves, you are marvelous and worthy of my attention. I respect you enough to make you the center of my universe for now.* When you give respect, a strange bounce effect occurs: if that leaf is valuable among the forest, you also are worthy of attention among the throngs of humans on earth.

Mount Hood National Forest, Oregon   August

I'm sitting outside the cabin, having done my morning rituals of fruit, chores, and back exercises. Since I'm on vacation I should be mellow, but instead, anxieties gnaw at my stomach.

A cobweb sparkling in the sun at the foot of a thick fir trunk snatches my mind away from my worries. Its lazy undulations remind me to slow down. The sweet scent of cedar and the soft air gently surround and calm me.

Since Sandra Jo has gone to town to call her daughter and to mail postcards, this might be a good time to play a game I've imagined but never tried. I call it "Crawl and Get Close." I'm wearing a sweater I can pull over my hands for protection if I need it. I could use gloves, I suppose, but I want to touch whenever possible. I'll crawl along the path to the parking spot. Since I walk that trail every day, it will be interesting to see in more detail what's along it.

First I crawl six feet to the base of the big fir. Dried needles on the trail poke my fingers a little, but it's tolerable. When I reach the trunk, I blow gently on a shimmering spider web that catches my eye. A foot away another spider sits in the center of its tidy round web. When I lie on the ground and tilt my head just so, I can see the sunshine light up the circles of silk, turning the web into a transparent phonograph record with rainbows playing across the ridges. I realize I could spend a long time in just this spot.

But I hear the car drive up and sure enough, Sandra Jo walks up and says, "What on earth are you doing?"

I explain the game I'm playing, and she's satisfied. "It just looks so odd," she says as she walks into the cabin.

Since she'll be sitting in front of the cabin reading soon, I'll change my route. I don't want even the smallest part of my mind worried about looking odd. I want to be alone with nature.

I go to the back of the cabin near the water

spigot. I'll crawl the path to the outhouse. For some reason I'm invested in getting farther than six feet this time. I want to crawl the whole path and find special spots I can then come back to and look at for a longer time.

After ten feet, I realize there is no outstanding magical spot here. When I'm this close, every square foot is magical. Getting close must be the universal antidote for boredom.

Shafts of light blink on and off between tree trunks, lighting first one miniature scene and then the next. At times like these I wonder why I bother driving great distances to visit natural wonders like waterfalls or the ocean. There are more wonders on this single path than I could explore in a month.

Even though I'm surrounded by beauty, I feel a need to go deeper. For me, this means stillness. I lean against a big fir root. The sword fern frond bobbing an inch from my chest holds a motley assortment of leaflets. Some are brown and curled into writhing shapes with teeth along their edges that look vicious. Some are green with beige and yellow spots.

Next to this mottled frond is one that's completely green and whole. No bug bites or tears mar its green health. They are the only two fronds of a single plant. I have no idea why they are so different.

I turn to the fern frond with curled brown leaflets. One leaflet catches the sun, so I focus there. It's ten inches from my face.

I have no agenda except to be still with it. I rest my gaze on it as I count my breaths to one hundred. As I become still inside, the leaflet becomes more vivid. Sharp black lines of shadow are cast onto its belly by the teeth along its own curved edge. What appeared to be solid brown is actually a multitude of shades melting into each other. Individual cells shine in the sun like the scales of a snake.

The fern hangs motionless in the sun; I lie motionless against the root. When I reach one hundred and can breathe with a still mind, I feel joy rush into my cells. The frond and I are both still and we're both silent. I'm happy to be with this plant.

I begin to chant Satnam silently in my mind so I won't get distracted by mind chatter. A voice inside my head says, *You don't need to do that. I'm real to you.* It's as though the leaf is saying I don't need to add anything artificial to keep the bond between us.

You are real to me, I say silently in my mind. The words are confirmed by the welling up of tears and joy. Actually, it's not just joy, but realness, that wells up. Are there words in our language for this feeling? *You are real to me.* The feeling is joyous, but not joy.

The feeling is recognition. I recognize the essence of the leaf. I accept its right to be; I respect its life. I feel a kinship with it, not because I'll die too, or because we share the same life process, but because it's real and so am I. It had a perfectly good life; it created exquisite serrated edges. It gave oxygen to the air and photosynthesized just as it was meant to. Its life was as real as mine. It's not dead because it was stupid or flawed. It had a perfectly good, full, busy, productive life. It's still real. It's flat and dry where I'm round and watery, but we're both real.

A tear runs into my nose and my back aches, but I'm not ready to leave yet. *Are you real because I love you?* I ask the leaf.

Love doesn't feel like the right word. *Are you real because I gave you fifteen minutes of attention, because I simply took the time to really notice you?* I think that's true. Realness is all around me. I just don't often stop to notice it or feel it.

I say, "You are real to me" to the sea of green leaves before me, but it rings false. I can feel the richness of life in them, but I think they can only be real to me one at a time.

I turn to the green fern frond. "You are real to me," I say. Yes, there is that feeling again. An energy seeps into me from the fern as every detail comes into sharp relief. It doesn't grow bigger in my sight, but the flow of energy from it to me becomes bigger. An invisible screen that I didn't even know was between us has dropped so that now more of its essence can reach me.

The air between the highest fir limbs and the plants down on the forest floor is thick with the energy and pulsing respiration of all this life. I am filled with this clear, nourishing soup.

Getting close to something in nature and focusing all your attention on it seems too simple to be powerful, but it's not. We rarely really look at the amazing world we're part of. When we look attentively, we receive more than we expect.

Julia Cameron, author of *The Artist's Way*, writes "The quality of life is in proportion, always, to the capacity for delight. The capacity for delight is the gift of paying attention."

Alan Watts goes one step further and says that really seeing leads to enlightenment:

> *Nor is the content of the liberation experience—* satori, nirvana, *"cosmic consciousness," etc.— something psychological in the sense of a flash of subjective light. Its content is the physical world, seen in a new way. . . . Eternity is now, and in the light of unrepressed vision the physical organism and the physical world turn out to be the divine world.*

You can reap the benefits of getting close to something natural almost anywhere. I've filled up on beauty by lying on the grass in my backyard and watching whatever was in front of my nose. I've felt a surge of friendliness toward a cactus in Seattle's conservatory greenhouse by putting my face inches from its curled spikes and sitting quietly with it.

Recently I was in a wheelchair after a foot operation, and my access to nature was limited. Once a day I went outside to wheel around the neighborhood. While I enjoyed rolling past the yards and gardens, I felt the deepest rejuvenation from sitting still as close as I could get to a bush overhanging the sidewalk. I immersed myself in the play of shadows across leaves and flower petals as the breeze made them dance; I stroked stems and sepals and twigs, letting my skin delight in their textures and aliveness. Those minutes spent with the bush stayed with me all day and for days afterward.

Getting close to something in nature is the easiest and quickest way to commune. You can do it in five minutes to reduce the stress of a busy day. Ten minutes will give you a mini-vacation that immerses you in beauty. With fifteen minutes and an open mind, you may tap into a sense of kinship with life that is comforting—even mystical.

Tips for Getting Close

1. Choose one thing to get close to and focus all your attention on it.
2. Get as close to that object or being as you can: sit, lie down, lean against it. Fill your whole visual field with it.
3. Touch that object or being.
4. Look for details.
5. Talk to that object or being.
6. Be still.

Sometimes you come to nature simply to rest. More often, you come to be changed, to grow. You hope for lessons and new perspectives and answers to nagging problems. In this chapter, you will discover one of the most effective ways to learn from nature: by communing with the role models it offers.

8
USING ROLE MODELS

When we were children, we read stories that encouraged us to use plants and animals as role models. "Be industrious like the ants; don't be lazy like the grasshopper. Be clever like the crow."

As adults, we might find it more difficult to be humble and say to nature, "Teach me. Show me how to live." And yet some of the most sacred literature instructs us to do just that. The Book of Job tells us

> *Ask now the beasts, and they shall teach thee;*
> *and the fowls of the air and they shall teach thee:*
> *Or speak to the earth, and it shall teach thee:*
> *and the fishes of the sea shall declare unto thee*

Dogen, one of the greatest masters of Zen Buddhism during the medieval period, wrote

> *There are all kinds of scriptures: some expound a*
> *sublime truth, others express a trivial reason. . . .*
> *Some indeed are written with the words of blades*
> *of grass or written with all kinds of trees.*

When we look to nature for lessons, when we ask, "What
can I learn from you?" we will find teachers everywhere.
During my first trip to the Canadian Rockies, I discovered
I could use almost anything as a role model. Everything
had wisdom to impart if I was willing to listen.

August

Yoho National Park, British Columbia, Canada

I sit in the middle of a dusty trail, looking down a
steep slope at the hoodoos: tall pillars of earth with
hard stone tops that have protected the pillars from
erosion. They stand high above the surrounding
bare ground. I ask if they have a message for me.

They reply, *We were deep in the earth; solid,*
secure, firm. We were part of the massive base from
which other things rose.

But everything changes. Life changes. We felt stable
being part of the ground. Now we're pillars: exposed,
alone, separate, and different from the earth mass

*below us. We never asked for this, or expected it, but
when change comes, you simply have to be yourself.
Even if it feels less secure, less known. Even if you stand
out. Life changes. We all respond to change differently.
It's all right to be unique.*

Whether or not we can put our questions into words, we all
yearn for, and unconsciously scan for, the lessons we need.
When I first saw the hoodoos, I had no idea I needed a lesson about accepting change. But it felt right when I heard it.

I like to think we have an internal healer, an internal teacher, and an internal nurturer that nudge us toward what we most need. When we look to nature for lessons, we hear exactly what we need to hear.

Lake Washington, Seattle   January

It's a beautiful morning at the lake. The sun is
warming me and lighting up the snow on the
Cascades. The lake is a rich turquoise. Occasionally
ducks or gulls fly by. The gentle lapping of the
waves soothes me and slows me down.

When I first came to the lake, people were
feeding bread to the geese and gulls down the shore.
The geese were dignified but grabby, the gulls were
screechy and combative. Now, breakfast is over, and

the whole colony of gulls is floating on the water. They aren't swimming; they're just slowly drifting east toward the empty center of the lake. Occasionally one washes itself or flies away, but mostly they simply float.

I feel as though I'm watching a morning meditation. It's as if the gulls were saying, *Yes, in every day there is a lot of busyness and screeching and feeding, but in every day there must also be floating, just floating. You must take time to be with the waves, the sun, and the bigness of the lake.*

They have been floating for a long time now. Watching them helps my mind relax and float with them. One minute, two minutes, five minutes pass. It seems as though I have been floating with them for an hour. I am relaxed and calm. They are right. In every day there must be time simply to float.

I never formally said to the gulls, "What do you have to teach me?" And the gulls never formally said back, "Here, learn this." Yet the lesson was there for the taking.

One of our barriers to learning from nature's role models is our reluctance to attribute human qualities to plants and animals. We may feel self-conscious when we assume we understand what floating means to a gull. After all, maybe those gulls were digesting or silently determining the pecking order for the day. Maybe floating isn't relaxing or serene for gulls at all.

When we're looking for lessons to help us in our own lives, the factual truth about gulls doesn't matter. Even naturalists won't ever understand gulls completely. What matters is that we look for any gift of learning we can receive as we watch them. It's up to our receptivity and creativity to find the examples and inspirations we need.

Never underestimate the power of a role model. Educational theories stress that what a teacher models has more impact than the content of the formal lesson.

Without knowing it, you use role models all the time. Do you gaze at floating clouds when you want to relax? It works, doesn't it? A friend of mine visits tall trees when he's depressed. He says they embody the upright principle of the universe and they make him feel like standing up straight.

Banff National Park, Alberta, Canada   August

I'm sitting at the end of Chephren Lake. Before me, Mount Chephren rises in beige rock tiers like an Egyptian pyramid.

Mount Chephren is not the only glorious peak here. The half-bowl mountain at the other end of the lake has dozens of smooth snowfields and a blue glacier that's tossing a stream of silver water down the rubble into the lake.

At my feet, that same water burbles back out of the lake after mingling with calm turquoise depths. Four feet from me is the final tree in a logjam at the lake's end. Here, on this floating trunk surrounded by rushing water, a community has decided to sprout.

While most of the other silvered logs are as naked as driftwood, this one trunk sprouts eleven clumps of grass, three clumps of miniature rushes, a wildflower patch, and a bonsai bush. Right now it's hard for me to identify with the magnificent pyramid of Mount Chephren or the liquid turquoise mirror of Chephren Lake, but I can relate to this small world on a dead trunk.

What amazes me is the integrity of this little community. It's so vibrantly alive. It blooms and produces seeds completely unaware of the danger rushing past on either side. Here, on a tiny doomed island, life flourishes as wholeheartedly as if it had been given the choicest meadow. It seems not at all disheartened by, or even aware of, its precarious base. The garden could be flooded out by a hot summer snowmelt, or the log could be set afloat to roll upside down against a muddy bank. The wood could simply rot away, water-logged and cracked open by the very roots that live upon it. None of the plants seems to care. This is the chance at life they are offered, and they're making something beautiful of it.

The plants on this log are great role models for me. I complain if I don't like the weather, or if my camper gets a flat tire, or if I can't spend enough time in nature. I don't often embrace life the way they do, grateful and openhearted, thrilled to make of this chance whatever they can make of it. I'm humbled by a log in a stream.

As I let nature teach me, I find that sometimes the examples are obvious. Be strong like the rock in the middle of the falls. Be flexible like the grasses bending in the wind. More often, however, the messages are subtle and surprising, as I describe in the next journal entry.

Behind the jungle gym in the playground down the street stands a small hill covered with plants and big, old trees. Although this "forest" is only about sixty yards by thirty yards, it's big enough to escape into. Multiple paths thread among the bushes, and when I see them, I wish every playground in the country had a miniature wilderness like this for children—and adults.

Leschi School, Seattle   September
   I'm in my menstrual-period state—slow, a little
   crampy, tired. Despite fearing that this lethargy

underlies a larger illness or terminal sloth, I wel-
come the slowness, the sense of limitations.

I managed to pack a lunch and drive here; my
choices now are to sit or lie down. Staring is a possible activity, as is breathing and leaning. Worrying
is always an option. But that's about it.

Hours of brilliant thought or helpful chores are
not open to me. I can't try for insights or rushes of
ecstasy from the life force. Insight and ecstasy, if
they come, will have to penetrate my mental fog on
their own initiative. I have no spare energy to cast
out like lines into the sea of wonder. I trudge
toward the trees.

Sun dapples huge trunks above soft brown earth
littered with leaves. Yes, this is a good nesting place.
I pile fallen leaves under my head for a pillow. They
crunch under my baseball cap as I lie back, setting
off an avalanche of smells—sweet, pungent, and
peppery.

Overhead, a maple cathedral arches. Its roof is
made of chartreuse and gold leaves that look like
stained-glass. Black snaking branches separate the
sparkling sections while a pale blue sky glows
between each pane. But it's not the dramatic
twisting branches, nor the bobbing glass leaves that
catch my soul; it's the huge, still expanse of air
under the branches. I take a deep breath.

Here my soul can stretch out into clear, arching space that's bounded only by beauty. Tiny birds flit through occasionally; a brown leaf spirals down and lands with a crunch. Mostly, nothing happens. Inside my heart, I'm as still as the thick brown trunk, letting myself simply be surrounded by beautiful spaciousness.

A red squirrel barks, a frog croaks. I silently speak to my tree, *What can I learn from you? You stand with such majesty, you twist with such grace. You create a space of beauty around you that you then get to live in. Does my heart react to you with pleasure because it wants me to create a space as lovely for it to live in?*

I can imagine the tree whispering back to me, *Stretch out your branches and paint your walls with glowing colors. Let only beauty and peace rest next to the core of you. Stand strong in the world, but keep softness and beauty as the air you breathe, the nourishment you draw from. Gnash your problems and pain out there between the teeth of your pointed leaves, but let only soft breezes ruffle your mossy trunk. Create space to contemplate your thoughts calmly as they drift to the ground one by one.*

Nature presents us with a huge range of role models.

Sometimes I'm drawn to a role model that reminds me of something I know I need in my life—the group of gulls reminded me to rest and meditate more often, for instance. Just as often, however, nature shows me possibilities I've never even thought of.

Before I lay under the big maple, I had never envisioned my core or considered that I needed space around it. But when I rested in the leaves and let myself be quiet, something clicked inside and said, *This feels wonderful. I want this in my life. What is this?*

When I use something unusual for a role model, two wonderful things happen: my vision for my life expands, and my sense of kinship with nature expands. Big maples are a little less alien. When I see one on the street now, a warm familiarity suffuses me.

Natural role models can enrich your daily life wherever you are. Ask the tree by the bus stop if it has a message for you. Ask the water in the irrigation ditch. Ask the philodendron on your windowsill. All you need is an open mind and a willingness to learn.

Stuart Udall, former U.S. secretary of the interior, encouraged Americans to learn from nature:

> *In recent decades we have slowly come back to some of the truths that the Indian knew from the beginning: that unborn generations have a claim on the land equal to our own; that men need to learn from nature, to keep an ear to the earth,*

and to replenish their spirits in frequent contacts with animals and wild land.

Tips for Using Role Models

1. Be willing to learn, to be humble, to be open. Be a student.
2. Notice what you're drawn to——it could be a plant, an animal, an object, or a scene.
3. Get close.
4. Let yourself wonder what draws you to a particular thing.
5. Notice how you feel as you focus on each thing.
6. With words or with your heart, ask, "What can you teach me?"

In this chapter, you will learn one of the quickest and easiest ways to commune. Being something natural——pretending you're a rock or a tree, for instance——lets you step out of your busyness mindset and step into a completely different reality. In one fell swoop, you settle in and merge, feel a sense of kinship, and experience a new perspective that may hold lessons for you. Being-it takes the use of a role model one step further, and it's fun, too!

9
BEING-IT

"Walk a mile in my shoes." This old familiar saying tells us we can't really know anyone else until we've lived a life like theirs. The exercise of being-it says the same thing. In order to know a rock, we have to live like a rock, be a rock.

The technique of being-it draws from many therapy traditions. Gestalt therapy encourages clients to sit in an empty chair and be the characters in their dreams or be parts of their own bodies like a fidgeting hand or a clenched jaw. In this way, clients can get inside the experience of the character or body part and see what message or wisdom it has to impart. Other therapy schools such as psychosynthesis, parts therapy, and voice dialogue suggest that clients sit in different chairs and be different parts of themselves—the wise part, the scared part, or the nurturing part, for instance. The client can get inside the feelings, needs, and perspectives of one part and even dialogue with other parts. Exercises from movement therapy, couple counseling, and conflict resolution training instruct clients to "become" their partner or someone they want to understand better. When they move and speak as that other person, they get an inside look at how that person might feel and think. In each case, when clients try to become some part of themselves or some other person, they get more complex and complete information. The total-body experience engages their physical senses, emotions, intelligence, and intuition in the quest to know.

New clients are often taken aback the first time I use a being-it technique. I put a chair across from them and say, "I'd like you to try something that might feel strange at first. Go sit in that chair and be your angry stomach (or your mother, or the scared part of you). Tell me what you think and feel as your stomach. Tell me what you need as your stomach." Once they get over feeling silly, they are amazed at how powerful the experience is and how much they learn.

Being something in nature can be just as powerful. First of all, it forces you to drop your busyness mindset right away. It takes you out of your head and into your senses.

You can't be a rock feeling the wind on your surface while worrying about your taxes.

Being-it throws you into a totally new reality to enjoy, explore, and learn from. In the process, you become more familiar with that rock, and a sense of kinship grows naturally.

It is written in the ancient Kaivalya Upanishad, "Who sees himself in all beings and in himself all beings sees, enters into the highest Brahman without any other reason." Lest we think *beings* means only human beings, Albert Schweitzer adds,

> *And because the Universal Soul dwells in all Being, it finds its own self again in all Being, in the life of plants as in the life of gods. This is the meaning of the famous* Tat twam asi *(That thou art thyself) of the Upanishads.*

In the next experience, you'll notice that I use some techniques you learned in earlier chapters. In conjunction with being-it, I count my breaths to keep me focused, and I ask for a message, just as I did in the chapter on using role models.

February

Joemma Beach Park, near Purdy, Washington

The late afternoon sun warms me as I walk with my

friend Mike along the wide sandy beach. The tide is low and silent.

We reach a spot where we can see the Olympic Mountains and Mike says, "I'd like to try one of your communing exercises."

He settles onto the sand and leans against an old, barnacled piling. I say to him, "Choose something and *be* it. Imagine you're that thing, then notice how you feel and how the world looks from that point of view. You might choose a rock, or a gull, or the bay itself."

He nods. I think to myself, *That wasn't much of an explanation. It should have been more detailed, more inspirational, or more poetic. How can he know what to do from that little description?*

He's calmly arranging his coat underneath him. He seems to have no questions.

I move to another piling, sit on my coat, and shove my scarf and gloves behind my back as a makeshift lumbar support. It takes no time at all for me to choose. I want to be a rock.

Before me is a sandy beach strewn with thousands of rocks. I choose a three-inch beige stone lying six feet in front of me. It has no distinguishing characteristics. It's not beautiful or remarkable, but it's close and easy to look at. I take a deep breath and imagine what I would feel if I were the rock.

As the rock, I'm very still and very solid. The sunny side of me feels warm, the shaded side is cool. Tiny gusts of wind tickle me with cold kisses. I'm heavy.

I feel at home here. This is where I live every day. I don't move from this spot. The sand around me may shift four times a day when it's my turn to be lapped by the incoming or outgoing tide, but even the sand doesn't move much. I sit here surrounded by thousands of rocks. I'm part of a multitude.

I'm vaguely aware of the water sloshing below me and the Olympic Mountains in the far distance, but I'm more keenly aware of being surrounded by space. My universe is the huge vault of blue air above and around me. I'm small, silent, and solid in the middle of this vastness.

The cries of nearby gulls are tiny vibrations that lap against me. As a rock, I'm undisturbed by their raucous bickering. I notice distant sounds and events, but I stay centered. I let the sounds and sights come to me; I do no reaching.

My human mind begins to wander. In order to keep my focus on being the rock, I count my breaths to one hundred and say *rock* to each count. *One, rock; two, rock; three, rock. . . .*

I alternate closing my eyes for ten counts and opening them for ten counts. When I close my eyes,

I feel the stillness inside. I feel heavy and dark. When I open my eyes I feel at home. I have a beautiful home. The distant mountains and the sweep of rocks down the beach are deeply familiar. I have no place to go and nothing to do. I can just be home. I can just be.

When I finish counting my breaths, I come back into being my human self and silently ask the rock if it has any message for me. Words spring into my mind in response. *You have within you the same solid stillness you feel in me. No matter the imagined urgency of your life, your core is always there, rock solid. That's why you like being me. You like to remember. You like to help your own solid stillness emerge again. Your core remembers the value of being grounded. You can be the rock part of you at any time. It's there as surely as all the other parts of you are there. You come to me to reawaken it. We're not so different.*

I feel a hard stillness in the core of my trunk that tingles like a smile. It's as strong and stable as the rock.

My back is stiff. No matter how much I'm enjoying communing, my body calls time. Hearing Mike stir, I move back to his piling and ask what he thought of the exercise.

He says, "I liked it. It was fun and it relaxed me quickly. Usually I resist guided meditations where the leader tells me to be a tree or something. The directions often distract me from my experience. But this time I could pick what I wanted to be and what I wanted to focus on. It was easy."

"What were you?" I ask, settling down beside him.

"I chose to be the little bay below us. I was the sand, and I could feel the water lapping against me. Then I noticed water seeping into me from above so I felt that, too. I kept noticing more and more about myself. Part of me was above the water and baking in the sun. Part of me had little rocks for the water to trickle over. I feel like I have a personal connection with that little bay now. I know that any time I want to I'll be able to remember how it looked and how I felt while I was being it."

I discovered this being-it method of communing during many visits to nature. At first, I often just sat in nature and tried to be quiet. I knew I wanted to commune, and I figured if I could get my body there, something would happen. Many times I couldn't turn my mind off, however, and I would end up feeling more tense and frustrated than when I began.

Sometimes lovely things did happen, and I noticed that those lovely things frequently happened after I found myself accidentally "being" something around me. Let me give you an example.

One Christmas, family and friends gathered at a cabin on Mount Hood. It wasn't the most conducive situation for communing with nature; it was freezing outside and noisy inside.

Nevertheless, I made a point of sitting out on the tiny glassed-in porch at least once a day to get some peace and quiet and to try to commune with nature. I was always bundled in layers of sweaters and a down coat; often I used my earplugs as well. It wasn't my favorite way of communing. I'd have preferred to be surrounded by the sounds and smells of the forest, but it was too cold. It was amazing to me that being-it worked even through glass and under such uncomfortable conditions.

Mount Hood National Forest, Oregon   December

I'm sitting in the sun on the cabin porch. I can feel the cold air on my face and see my breath when I let out a deep exhale. I'll have only a short time out here today.

Moss-draped maples shine in the sun along the creek in front of the cabin. Huge cedars stand as the perfect dark-green backdrop.

Muffled sounds from the house tickle my curiosity, but I'm not distracted for long. The big open space over the stream draws my attention like a magnet. It looks like a roundish amphitheater of space.

I imagine myself the shape of the space. I'm full and round, relaxed and open. I can feel twigs and branches reaching into me; I can feel the air and sun circulating freely through me.

At my edges, I go on forever, sifted through branches and needles and tufts of moss—now sifted finely, now surprised by sudden open spaces. I can feel the transfer of nutrients from me to the trees and back from the trees. I'm thrilled by birds winging through me and leaves floating down. Being space is lovely.

I come back to myself and focus on the network of icy silver twigs that hang inches from my window. Highlighted against the shadowed hillside across the creek, they look like crystal cobwebs cutting through space.

I ask myself which branch I identify with. When I find the simple branch that's "me," my whole body relaxes in response. It has few junctions or offshoots; it's thick enough to be both sturdy and supple. I start to feel as though I'm the branch.

As the branch, it's easy to be simple. My spare lines center me and bring me back into my own basic self. When I look at the other branches in their complexity, I feel tense and scattered. I really do want a simple life.

I can see now why people who follow some spiritual traditions meditate on certain objects—a candle, a rock garden. Perhaps they want some of the essence of those things, or perhaps they simply want help activating what is already inside themselves. The space over the creek opens me up, loosening my tight edges. The branch affirms my need for simplicity, letting me feel that need on a visceral, rather than on an intellectual, level.

You'll notice I didn't decide in advance to do a being-it exercise; it just happened. Back then, I doubt that I even knew what I was doing that made the experience so special. Now that I know, I can choose to be something anytime I want.

It would be rational and tidy if I simply said to myself, "Oh, today I feel scattered, I think I'll be a rock." Or, "Today I feel tense, it would probably relax me to be the space over the creek." Communing is never quite so tidy, however. What my rational brain thinks I need may not be what I need at all. It's far more powerful to simply wait and see what I'm drawn to. If I start to be something and it doesn't feel quite right, I try something else.

When I notice what I'm drawn to, I get valuable information about what I need in my life. If I'm drawn to a simple branch and experience the pleasure of simplicity by being that branch, I may make a commitment to simplify my life when I get back home.

I often find myself being a rock when I need stillness. I get a sense of peace from gathering my energies together in one place and not wandering.

When I'm tense, I may be drawn to being space or a whole scene. Then my peace comes from being huge and diffuse—like mist.

Both rock and space sensations are very different from my busyness mindset. A busy mind neither lands anywhere long enough to feel the peace of really being there, nor lets go long enough to relax into not being in control.

One of the joys of communing is that you never know what you will experience or what you will learn. Gregory Bateson commented,

> To increase awareness of one's scientific universe is to face unpredictable increases in one's aware-ness of self. And I wish to stress the fact that such increases are always in the very nature of the case unpredictable in nature. . . . No one knows the end of that progress which starts from uniting the perceiver and the perceived—the subject and the object—into a single universe.

You can be a simple object, like a rock or a twig. You can be something more complex, like part of a bay or the space over a creek. Let yourself be open to unusual possibilities.

This is a chance to stretch yourself and experiment. One day in Seattle, for instance, I became the color green.

Washington Park Arboretum   May

Summer green and robin calls surround me in this little meadow. I bring a whirling mind to the peace here—should I buy a new transmission for my van? But the van's so old, it may not be worth the expense. Should I sell it? But it's so comfortable for me and I love it.

I need this meadow to drive out the feeling that life is all chores and impossible decisions. I need to *be* here quickly and completely.

From every direction, the color green streams into my eyes. All this green feels like a massive transfusion of real life into my hungry soul. Warm sun and a gentle breeze soften my flesh so I can absorb more and more, deeper and deeper.

I imagine my skin, my fat, my muscles, my sinews all green. I feel my organs thrumming a deep green tone. My bones are the last to grant entrance. Slowly the green tint seeps into their pure ivory, making my bones pale green clear to the marrow.

I need this total immersion. I need to be permeated and taken over completely. I'm green. I'm here now. Here is green.

The wind passes first around me, then around the mossy green maple trunk behind me. One fly lands on the shoulder of a bent piece of grass; another rubs its front legs together on my shoulder. A few colors float through our greenness—yellow butterfly, black crow, red-eyed fly.

Now that I'm green, there is nothing urgent to do. Green is slow. Green is tranquil.

Green lies heavily on the ground, rooted. Green has no desires. I wear lethargy without a struggle.

Eventually, I rouse myself to take a walk. "I am green. I am just like you; I am green," I chant as I walk. Each time I chant I feel a tightness leave me and a sense of oneness with the park come over me.

"I am green. I am just like you." I belong here, too.

A teenage boy bicycles past. A middle-aged man jogs by. Green never hurries that much. Green walks or sits or lies down.

I walk through the parking lot. A panicky feeling pushes me to stride faster across the concrete. I feel uncomfortable when so much green has been paved over. I'm glad to reach the grass at the edge of the lot. "I am green. I am just like you."

Whenever my mind wanders, a wall of separateness rebuilds itself stealthily until I retrieve my attention and pin it back onto the words. I focus on one plant at a time. "I am green; I am just like you,"

I say to stalks of grass. Yes, I can feel myself as straight and tall as the slim blades.

"I am green; I am just like you," I say to the bright new tips of a fir. As the fir, I can feel the sun pouring into my cells while I hang in the air.

When I speak to each plant, I smile with the aliveness I feel. Each green is different. Each green keeps me centered here and now until I reach the metal box of my van. This green person, unfortunately, has to go to work.

Being something that's everywhere—like the color green—triggers a different kind of kinship. It's not the friendship-like kinship you might feel toward a specific tree or even toward a particular species of tree, it's kinship with the whole of life. Albert Einstein said our task was to free ourselves from the "optical illusion" that we are separate from the rest of the universe:

> A human being is part of the whole that we call the universe, a part limited in time and space. He experiences himself, his thoughts and feelings, as something separated from the rest—a kind of optical illusion of his consciousness. This illusion is a prison for us, restricting us to our personal desires and to affection for only the few people nearest us. Our task must be to free ourselves from

this prison by widening our circle of compassion to
embrace all living beings and all of nature.

By using the exercise of being-it, we can widen our circle of empathy and compassion bit by bit. First we may find parts of nature less scary and alien, then more friendly, and finally, more like family.

Being-it is a great exercise to use at home. If I bring that rock home from the beach, I can set it in front of me and be it again. Or I can close my eyes, remember that branch, and be it again. I'm always surprised how many of the sensations I can remember and how refreshed I feel.

I can also be any rock on the street. Each stone has a long history and an essence worth meeting, no matter where it rests at the moment. Street rocks might not seem wild enough to commune with, but they are. The rocks on my street were carried here by a huge glacier millennia ago, a fact I remember when I become them.

It's hard to commune through a window because the sensations from smell and touch and hearing are cut off. Being-it lets me evoke the sensations I can't receive directly. When I become the fir branch beside my living room window, I feel the wind as I bob.

Being something that surrounds me is another good exercise to use in any setting. I can be green on my walk to the library, or be a cloud on a rainy day downtown, or be the air in a parking lot. Each time I can get that full body rush of reconnecting with nature.

Try being something natural right now. Find a nearby plant or stone or use the air around you. Then be it and see what happens.

Tips for Being It

1. Close your eyes and imagine what your surroundings look like from the point of view of the object you've decided to be. If you're a stone, you might be aware of trees looming high overhead and grass nearby that's just your size. If you're a tree, you might imagine looking down on the tiny plants below.
2. Notice the sounds around you.
3. Notice the sensations you feel: air temperature, wind, and sun.
4. Notice the smells.
5. Imagine what it feels like to be the size and shape and density of your object. As a stone, what is it like to be heavy and dense and still? As a tree, what does it feel like to be tall, to have your arms outstretched, and to sway in the breeze?
6. Open your eyes and keep moving from sense to sense. What else do you see? What else do you feel? Does grass blow against you? Does a bird land on one of your branches?

7. You can try to keep your mind silent, or you can use the words in your mind to narrate your experience and keep you focused: *I feel heavy; I hear a robin warbling.*

8. You can say your name with each breath: "One, stone; two, stone; three, stone. . . .

9. Once you've experienced being something in the present moment, the possibilities are endless. You can imagine the stone's life throughout the day or throughout the year. You can talk to the tree's neighbors or ask the tree a question. You can even ask for advice about a problem you may have.

In this chapter, you will bring together techniques you have learned in previous chapters that will help you reach for the essence of your communing experience. You will also expand the technique of being-it by asking yourself, *What is the essence of this object or place? What is its revelation for me?* Then you can distill your discovery into a few power-packed words and create a mantra you may use for years.

10
REACHING FOR THE ESSENCE

In his first book, *Nature,* Ralph Waldo Emerson posed a challenge:

> *The foregoing generations beheld God and nature face to face; we, through their eyes. Why should not we also enjoy an original relation to the universe? Why should not we have a poetry and philosophy of insight and not of tradition, and a religion by revelation to us, and not the history of theirs?*

When you commune with nature, you bring yourself face to face with "God and nature," making a personal revelation possible. By using the techniques you have learned, you can purposefully seek the most powerful revelation a particular place in nature holds for you. After settling in, becoming present, finding a role model and being it, you can ask, *What touches me most deeply here?* and *What is the essence of that which touches me?*

In the process of trying to answer those questions, you are reaching for the essence of your experience, always searching for the physical resonance in your core that tells you your answer rings true. Then you can distill your answer into key words and create a mantra that may keep teaching you and connecting you with nature for a long time.

Revelations don't come on demand, of course. They are always a gift. But techniques you have learned will help you be open and receptive, will help you probe for deeper meanings, and will help you put the revelations you do encounter into words you can use again and again. Over time, this experience and these words can become part of your "philosophy of insight" and "religion by revelation"— what you know about life based on your own experience.

In the communing experience that follows, I didn't know at the beginning that I wanted a revelation, I only knew I wanted a heart connection with nature. You will recognize the techniques I used. I counted my breaths to settle in and I used silence to be present. I chose my role models and used the technique of being-it to make a heart connection with each one. I used words to probe the essence of each role model I was being and then distilled those words into a mantra. Using the mantra a few times added the final word to the revelation.

Banff National Park, Alberta, Canada   July

It's 7:30 A.M. I sit before a crystal waterfall and a bubbling turquoise pool at Johnston Canyon. Mist swirls up while tiny drops of rain arrow down.

I want to feel connected and in love with life, but I don't. Perhaps I can't connect because I know dozens of other tourists will soon descend upon me. Perhaps it's simply hard for my heart to open to the rush and roar of a falls. I can relate to a still lake, a flower, or even a cliff. I can imagine being them. But I'm never as powerful and outrageous as a waterfall, so a falls always seems more alien.

I count my breaths to twenty; I go silent inside. I imagine being one with the falls. Phew! What an adrenaline rush! I feel as though I'll burst apart from the sheer energy of it.

I breathe deeply. I let myself notice whatever happens while I become the falls. Soon being that roaring cataract actually begins to feel more familiar. I think of the ways in which I'm like the falls.

I'm as powerful and clear as the falls in my love

for the earth. I'm clear about loving being a therapist and a writer. As I name my passionate loves one
by one I feel more kinship with the falls. I, too,
know the delicious, scrubbed-clean rush of certain
love.

Now there is a smile in my chest instead of a
repulsion. I'm like you in some ways, falls. I do con-
tain that power and sureness sometimes.

A cascade of delight pours down my torso. What
a thrilling feeling: unambivalent love.

I begin to feel blasted open. The cells inside my
trunk are giggling silently.

After twenty minutes by the falls, I continue my
hike. The trail steepens and comes out at an
orange-and-black, slick, travertine cliff that's so
huge it fills my whole view. A crystal green creek
tumbles at its feet like a pack of puppies playing at
the feet of a dozing dinosaur.

After feeling the rush of the lower falls flowing
through me, I'm taken aback by this wall. Instead of
being perpendicular, it slopes gently like a billowing
drape. Three slender rivulets fan out into shining
sheets that wash its whole bulk. Although the water
slides down the wall, it could never be called a falls
or a powerful torrent of love.

This water spreads its love evenly over its wall,
over its life. Every inch of travertine is dripping,

alive, loved, stroked, fed. Here is a different model.
Bulges in the rock easily look like breasts and a
belly, shoulder blades and the curve of the spine. I
can imagine being this wall, and feeling the water
love every inch of my skin, every wart and scar,
every roll of fat and bulge of muscle.

All of my self is loved every minute on this wall.
All of my self is renewed and attended to. Here is
the Buddhist moment-to-moment attention.
Awareness spreads out to encompass all of life—not
just the goals and loves, but the rubble and the
algae as well.

My body relaxes from the high energy rush it had
gotten from the big lower falls. Some of my awareness moves from the torrent in my core and spreads
through my limbs and skin. This is another way to
be in love, another way to love life.

I sigh and feel my skin warm and tingle as I
spread my energy to the edges of myself. I take a
deep breath and wrap the water's caressing energy
around me. Like a flannel robe, it comforts my arms
and shoulders, it swirls around my belly and legs.

I walk to the edge of the slick travertine wall and
face the vertical black cliff beside it. Stillness sinks
into me with a thunk. The black rock is stark and
square and still.

I move a few steps farther down the path and say

157

hello to the thundering cataract of the upper falls. It is lovely and compelling. I love that fierce, focused passion.

I turn slowly from the travertine drape to the still cliff to the roaring falls. I want this vibrant skin of awareness, this solid black structure of silence and peace, and this torrent of crystal passion in my life.

I look at the blocky black wall between the roaring upper falls and the glistening travertine. *Peace is not a strong enough word to describe you,* I tell it. *You are grounded in rock-solid knowing. I'll call you reality.*

My gaze drops to the creek. I should include it in my scenario. It represents the energy of letting go. At my feet, all the energy simply flows away. I want these four to be cornerstones of my life: the awareness of the slick travertine, the rock-solid reality of the cliff, the passion of the falls, and the ability to let go like the creek.

Families clomp by, rattling the metal catwalk I perch on. Rain comes and goes. None of these perturb me. Finally my feet and back are too sore to stay longer, so I say good-bye to the walls and falls.

Wild rose and pine scents pour over me as the trail enters the forest. I chant my new mantra slowly: *Awareness, reality, passion, letting go.*

Awareness feels like an alive skin. Reality feels like

straight, solid bones. Passion is an excitement cascading deep inside my rib cage. Letting go is swirling water that makes my feet tingle. As I chant, my attention moves from my skin to my bones and rib cage, then down and out my feet. The sensations are delightful.

Farther down the trail I chant, *Awareness, reality, passion, letting go. Awareness, awareness; reality, reality; passion, passion; letting go, letting go.* I chant each word three times, then four times.

It's particularly nice to chant on this plain, forested part of the path where my mind might wander or get dull. I chant simply *Awareness* for a while, and a funny clunk happens in my chest. My sense of my body in space and my vision all seem to shift a quarter of an inch, and suddenly I feel at home.

I'm not "aware" of these canyon walls as different from me, or even as an analogy for myself and my life. We're simply all here together, all at home together. I add "home" to my mantra. *Awareness, reality, passion, letting go, home.* I sigh. My shoulders relax. My lungs suck in a deep breath. Now I'm aware of home and of being at home.

Shafts of sun bake wet pine needles. The scent is so spicy it reminds me of the hot chaparral smells of southern California.

I return to the lower falls. Passion roars through a

life that's held tightly by solid reality and carpeted with soft, glistening awareness. All the excess energy dances away. This is my home.

Reaching for the essence of a communing experience may take longer than you expect. On a single trail, nature offers many role models to choose from. After you've found the place or the quality you want to focus on, it takes time to settle in, be present, be it, probe it with words, and distill its essence into a mantra. It may seem like work, but the process itself will bring you more and more in tune with nature the longer you spend with it. And the intensity of the effort burns the feelings and insights into your nerve pathways so they can be recalled more easily once you're back in your daily life.

Poets know the delicious feeling that comes with finding just the right word to match what they want to say. Reaching for the essence of a communing experience is very much like composing a haiku poem. You're trying to match words to the core of your experience in nature. When you keep trying different descriptions and words, you'll eventually find the ones that produce a right response in your body—a deep breath, a tingling of energy, a smile, tears. If you stay in touch with how you feel as you repeat a word, you may find that a truer word emerges, as I did when the "peace" of the black cliff became "reality." You may use a particular mantra for just an hour to deepen your experience, or you may use it over and over for years.

Sometimes it takes a vacation in a national park to inspire a revelation you will remember for life. Sometimes it takes that stunning beauty to penetrate your habitual ways of relating to the world, and it takes extended time to shed the layers of your busyness mindset so you are open enough to receive profound insight. Communing for long periods in piercingly magnificent settings can touch your deepest self. By reaching for the essence of your experience and creating a mantra at one of those moments, you have something to bring home that will help sustain you in your ordinary life. Months or even years later, using that mantra during quick breaks in your own backyard will help you get into the deeper and more refreshing levels of communing more quickly.

Seattle   January

I'm lying in a spot of sun in a friend's backyard.
The air is chilly, but the sunlight is warm. Frost
glows from the deep shade.

Most of the yard is taken up by a huge redwood
tree, but just here, in front of the tree, the grass is soft
and the sun-warmed redwood leaves spice the air.

I admire the blue sky-shards shining through the

branches and smile at the shadows that dance on the deep red trunk. Just watching isn't taking me as deep as I want to go, though, so I begin to chant, *Awareness, awareness.* Immediately my skin tingles and the air becomes crystal clear; all the edges sharpen and the colors shout. *Reality, reality,* I continue. My body feels heavy on the mat as the unseen world of molecules and physical laws looms huge in my consciousness. *Passion, passion,* I whisper to the thick trunk and the sparkling air. A surge of love washes through my cells and wakes up my skin. *Open heart, open heart,* I chant as I imagine my chest opening and all my skin peeling back to fearlessly let this world touch me. Now I tingle all over and feel the deep relaxation that comes with dropping defenses and boundaries. I am wide open to the living earth. *Letting go, letting go,* I tell myself. Some internal grasping releases, my stomach relaxes, and I can let nature simply be. *Home, home,* I finish. There, there's the final relaxation—the comfortable feeling of being embedded in this world, of being effortlessly held and nourished. Now I am both deeply relaxed and completely alert, at one with my environment and clearly myself. Now I am home.

Even though I had the revelation and created the mantra six years before I used it in my friend's yard, it could still take me deep into myself and deep into relationship with nature. Over the years I have used it in many settings and have added the words *open heart*. This mantra has become an old friend.

You won't always need days in the wilderness to reach the essence of an experience or to create a mantra. You can go deeper into a communing experience anywhere by asking yourself a simple question that begins, *What is the essence of . . . ? What is the essence of this place? What is the essence of what I feel now? What is the essence of what I need now?*

You don't have to be a poet or a meditation master to distill your revelation into words that capture that essence. You're the expert on the phrases that touch your own heart. Experiment!

Tips for Reaching for the Essence

1. Be a place or a thing in nature and ask yourself any of the following questions, or just ask one of these questions after you have settled in somewhere:
   a. *How would I describe the essence of this place or thing in a word or a few words?*
   b. *How do I feel in this place or as this thing? Are there one or two words that can capture what I feel?*

   c. *What lesson does this place or thing have for me? Are there one or two words that can distill the lesson so I can repeat it and take it home with me?*

   d. *What would I like to focus on here? What is my intention? What word or words can I repeat to keep me zeroed in?*

   e. *Is there a sound, or a set of sounds, that expresses the essence of this place or how I feel here? Sometimes sounds work as well as words that carry meaning.*

2. After you've asked yourself the question you've chosen, try out words one at a time. You will know if you've found the right words or sounds when your body reacts with a feeling of "rightness."

3. Repeat your mantra to keep yourself present and to deepen your experience.

Communing can help you "come home" to nature and to yourself. If you feel awkward going to nature, take along this chapter's summary of quick tips. It will make your homecoming easier.

11
COMING HOME

Several years ago, my friend Joan decided to go to an isolated hot springs to celebrate her fortieth birthday. It was a quest of sorts, a time to look back at the first half of her life and dream about the second half, a time to reconnect with herself and with the earth. She was pretty nervous. She hadn't spent much time in nature alone, and she was afraid she'd get out there and not know what to do with her time. She was afraid she wouldn't feel at home.

Since she didn't want to carry a whole book of exercises in her backpack, I wrote up a summary sheet for her. She read it first thing in the morning and last thing at night. She referred to it anytime she needed some reassurance or guidance. It became a companion and a touchstone.

If spending time alone in nature is new or awkward for you, if you've been away from it for a long time and aren't sure you'll remember what to do, carry this summary with you. Whether you go up the block or up the mountain, make your visit home to nature as easy and as fun for yourself as you can.

The 8 Basic Steps for Communing are

1. *Decide* to commune.
2. Set aside your busyness mindset.
3. Step into your communing mindset.
4. Focus on your goals and intentions.
5. Settle in and relax.
6. Use silence to clear your mind and heighten your awareness.
7. Point yourself in a particular direction by starting with an exercise or a goal, or start with an open mind and an attitude that lets you be receptive to whatever happens.
8. Bring back something from your most important experiences that can nourish your ordinary life—a mantra, an image, or a bit of writing.

Nature can be

—*an unfamiliar, fascinating culture*
Don't expect to be comfortable right away. Realize you

may have a lot to learn and may be awkward and do things wrong. You will have fears.

Take your essential creature comforts with you wherever you go. This culture can't provide the kinds of things you are used to having. My essentials are rain gear or a sun hat and sunblock, mosquito repellent, water and snacks, tissues, and a big plastic bag in case I need to sit someplace wet or muddy.

Be curious about everything you see. Why is the ecosystem set up this way? Why is the bug that color?

—*your body's home*

This is the place to find your body's true rhythms without society's schedules or expectations. Do you want to nap six times a day? Eat seven times a day? Stretch or walk or jump? When do you need stimulation and when do you need to put a pillow over your head and pull all your antenna back inside?

—*a role model*

Meditate on a rock. Can you become that silent and still inside? Meditate on a cloud or blowing grass. Can you be that flexible and light inside? What personal quality do you want to develop? Find something in nature that has that quality and be it.

—*a playmate*

No one is watching. Be wild. Crawl, dance, tell the trees jokes, be a tree and sway when it does. Lie down in the grass and feel it poke through your shirt. Let a fly crawl on your arm and feel it tickle you as it travels. Walk barefoot. Build with mud and stones. Throw water in the air and watch it sparkle.

—*a place to make new friends*

Get close to one thing and spend time with it. Find something that attracts you and be it. You'll feel like you're surrounded by friends.

—*a place to be yourself*

You don't have to meet anyone else's expectations here. You can simply be yourself, noticing who you are as you change moment to moment.

You can focus on your own goals. What do you want from your time in nature? Write a list of your hopes and intentions and refer to it every day.

—*a teacher*

Ask any scene, event, animal, plant, or object what it has to teach you. Quiet your mind and see what you learn by simply being receptive. Dialogue with the scene or object—question, answer, disagree, laugh.

—*a place to expand your mind*

You can break away from your traditional ways of thinking and find new perspectives. Talk to something very old or very young, very big or very small. Be something unusual, like a whole canyon or a pile of fallen branches. Challenge your imagination.

—*a place to ask the Big Questions*

Now that you're away from the consuming details of

your daily life, ponder the meaning of life and death and love and pain. Wonder about the purpose of your life and how you fit into the grand scheme of things.

—*a place to feel at home*

You can relax here. Sit in a place where you are surrounded by only beauty and natural sounds. Notice how restful it is to let go of the barriers you unconsciously hold up to block out the ugly, noisy parts of civilization. Practice relaxing deeply. Notice everything that nourishes you. Let your cells memorize the feeling of being at home; this memory can act as true north and pull the arrow of your inner compass back anytime you wander too far away.

You can use the exercises in this book for a quest of your own. In the book *Profiles in Wisdom*, Native elder Medicine Story says we all need to quest for our sense of home and our purpose here:

> *The Original Instructions urge us to find our place in the cosmos, to know our true nature and our goal in existence. There must be a response—not an intellectual answer—but a felt understanding of the nature of this existence, of its purpose and of our part in that purpose. That is the reason for the spiritual quests, the religions, the rituals, the searches, pilgrimages, meditations, and mystic*

> *disciplines of humankind. Something in our con-*
> *sciousness is just not satisfied with only eating,*
> *sleeping, creating, and reproducing. Something in*
> *us wants to know what it's all about and how we*
> *fit into it.*

We're on some kind of quest during every stage of our life cycle. There are always new things to learn and tasks to accomplish as we grow. The success of our quests may depend on communing with nature.

In our childhoods, nature offers an infinite store of tiny friends and wonders. Our small nervous systems and brains thrive on its complex, organic stimulation. In our adolescence, nature offers the challenges we need to prove ourselves and hone our skills. It provides a comfortable place away from peer pressure where our developing ideas about aesthetics and values can blossom. In young adult-hood, nature offers a place to release the stresses of our busy lives. When we touch our bare feet to the soil, we can remember the quiet core of ourselves and can ask the big questions about our place in this amazing universe. As older adults, we can turn to nature for rest and comfort and inspiration. We can build deep supportive friendships with plants and favorite spots based on familiarity, and we can integrate nature into all aspects of our lives—spiritual, mental, emotional, and physical.

Throughout the years, nature teaches us about reciproc-ity and interdependence. Nature is a home that everyone contributes to, and, unfortunately, a home that most of us feel estranged from these days.

Historian Thomas Berry echoes the feeling many of us have about our lives when he writes

> *We are returning to our native place after a long absence, meeting once again with our kin in the earth community. For too long we have been away somewhere, entranced with our industrial world of wires and wheels. . . .*
>
> *. . . the wilderness world recently rediscovered with heightened emotional sensitivity, is an experience not far from that of Dante meeting Beatrice at the end of the* Purgatoria, *where she descends amid a cloud of blossoms. It was a long wait for Dante, so aware of his infidelities, yet struck anew and inwardly "pierced," as when, hardly out of his childhood, he had first seen Beatrice. The "ancient flame" was lit again in the depths of his being. In that meeting, Dante is describing not only a personal experience, but the experience of the entire human community at the moment of reconciliation with the divine after the long period of alienation and human wandering away from the true center.*
>
> *Something of this feeling of intimacy we now experience as we recover our presence within the earth community.*

Most of us are coming home after a long absence. We have been away too long, and now we are returning home to the aliveness and nourishment of nature, and home to our essential selves. Both the natural and the internal home-comings are crucial to our well-being, and both can be reached by communing with nature.

Communing lets us feel in our bones how we are related to and connected with our large family of plant and animal siblings, how we are embedded in and nourished by the natural environment just as surely as an embryo is embedded in a womb. Communing opens the doors to the deep still place inside and helps us feel comfortable in our internal home.

Our natural home and our inner home have a fascinating relationship. We can reach both homes by heading toward either one. If we focus on natural role models and rhythms, we find ourselves feeling centered. If we focus on our quiet inner core, we find ourselves feeling at one with the universe.

Whenever I come home in nature, I feel grateful to the people in the generations before me who preserved the environment and saved some wild places. When I commune in a park, I particularly appreciate Rachel Carson and everyone who still helps push our nation toward sound environmental practices. Because of her, I have not had to face a silent spring. Because of her, the chirps of birds and insects let me know my family is around me wherever I am.

When I commune in the wilderness, I especially appreciate John Muir and everyone who still helps preserve wild land. Because of him, my siblings and I have magnificent places to call home.

John Muir knew about the convergence of our outer and inner homes. He wrote: "I only went out for a walk and finally concluded to stay out till sundown, for going out, I found, was really going in."

EPILOGUE

Ten years after my first three-week trip to the Canadian Rockies, I went back for three months. I wanted enough time to steep myself in its magnificence and to bask in its beauty. The trip didn't turn out quite the way I had hoped.

That summer broke the record for rainfall and nearly broke the record for cold temperatures. On top of that, I sprained my back so that my activities were severely limited and often invaded by pain. Fortunately, I had spent the ten intervening years teaching myself how to commune. Nature didn't have to create the perfect conditions for me to experience rapture. I walked the short trails and sat in a beach chair; I brought a raincoat and a hot water bottle. I communed in the short breaks between rainstorms; I found bliss in the cracks.

One of my favorite spots was Mount Edith Cavell, a mountain with a nearly perpendicular rock face. At its foot lies the small blue Cavell Glacier which has retreated over the years and left behind a valley of rocks and a milky pond. On Mount Edith Cavell's shoulder hangs another glacier—Angel Glacier—that periodically drops ice chunks that thunder down the mountain.

Visiting Mount Edith Cavell many times gave me the opportunity to experience the love that comes from familiarity. When my three months were up, I went to see it for one last time.

Jasper National Park, Alberta, Canada   August

I'm alone on a plain of golden boulders. I'm alone in the bowl of air exhaled all night by Mount Edith Cavell and its family of ridges and glaciers. I chant as I walk: "I breathe your spirit into mine, ahey ahey ahey ahey; I breathe my spirit into yours, aho aho aho aho." I chant, "My cells drink in your sweetest air, ahey ahey ahey ahey." The chants help me stay focused when I walk, but when I stop, I crave silence. My open chest and my open cells suck in the huge, still grandeur.

I set up my beach chair beside the meltwater pond at the base of the mountain. Tomorrow I leave Jasper. I don't know how to commune here for the last time. I don't know how to say good-bye.

The moraine to my left is as tall as a hill. I run my eyes down its rocky slope to a big gray-splotched boulder beside me and keep myself there for five breaths. The boulder and I rest together above the lovely, green, glacier-fed pond. I slide my eyes to an orange flat-topped boulder. For five breaths, tears well at its beauty. *I love you, boulder.*

I move my gaze to a tiny fir tree. Tears roll down

my face. *I love and respect you, beautiful, courageous fir.*

I let my eyes rove from the tree to a grass clump. *I can feel the soft swaying of your graceful drooping grass-heads. My chest softens as I count five breaths with you.*

Each tiny visit of five breaths touches my heart and reminds me how I've loved these beings. During other visits I've meditated with each one of them and felt a sense of kinship.

I run my eyes across the water to an ice floe. *I've watched you drip and melt; I've seen you glow turquoise and lilac and peach. You will be gone almost as soon as I leave.*

I run my eyes to the center of the pond and spend five breaths floating in the reflection of Cavell Glacier. I can feel the greens and golds and blues ripple through me. I imagine drifting onto the flat blue face of Cavell Glacier. I imagine stroking its crevasses and sliding my hand over its folded face. I catch my breath at its beauty.

I run my eyes up the cliff behind the glacier to spend five breaths with the falls and five with Angel Glacier and five with the black faces etched into the belly of the rock mountain. I let my body remember spending time with each one. I have no picture memories or word memories, but my skin and muscles and chest react to each. Each one has touched me differently. Each one feels familiar as it sets off the cells and feelings inside me that are its signature in my body. This loose tingling in my chest is the falls. This smile and quick inhale is Angel Glacier. This deep sigh and gaping mouth with stillness is the stark mountain.

My eyes return the way they came and I say, "I love you" to the mountain faces, Angel Glacier, the falls, Cavell Glacier, the pond, the floe, the grass, the tree, the flat boulder, and the gray rock. Then I close my eyes to commune.

Within five breaths I'm completely present. I had forgotten how distracting eyesight can be. I'm no longer fragmented, focusing here or there in the scene. Now I'm part of the whole place at once. The cold air pushing against my left cheek and filling my lungs is the air that fills this mountain bowl. The sounds of clunking rocks and roaring falls fill the whole space as well. I'm part of the bowl, surrounded by the same air and sounds, as still as a rock.

I open my eyes after fifty breaths to face Cavell Glacier. There are no words in English to describe what it is to me. A friend? No, that's too human. Something I love? Yes, but that can't describe the deep softness and piercing passion I feel toward it. I've meditated with it. I've been still with it. We've witnessed the pond and falls and floes and mountain together. It has always been there. It has always been beautiful.

We are parallel. I sit on this side of the pond below the mountain; it sits on that side. It's not like me in any way, really. It lives here; I visit. And yet, I feel such a heart connection with it. I smile whenever I look at it. I can't help myself. I love it fiercely and tenderly and chest-breakingly.

For fifty breaths I meditate while gazing at Cavell Glacier. This is not an empty, peaceful meditation. Tears pour down my cheeks and my heart pounds. I suck air into a chest that's bursting. I don't think or speak. Surges of joy and pain break loose from my heart and ripple through my body as I'm simply still with this entity I've come to love.

I close my eyes at fifty breaths and am glad I've learned how to meditate adequately with my mouth open because my nose is stuffed up. I sink back into the world of rumbling sound and kissing air. My tears fade and my chest stops aching. I melt again into being all of it at once. Just another rock. Just another member of the family.

After fifty breaths I open my eyes. I cannot maintain my silence. I want to tell Cavell Glacier what it has been to me. I want to say good-bye. But now, even though I want to talk, I have no words.

You're everything to me, I tell it. I can say *"I love you" but that only scratches the surface. Unfortunately, love is the biggest word we humans have.*

I wish I could write a whole dictionary of words for love. I would like to have a word for the love I feel toward a magnificent turquoise glacier I've communed with several times. That love encompasses the glacier's huge age and size, its beauty, its stillness, and the sense of it presiding over the pond and birthing ice floes. It includes the warmth of being in the home of a beloved one, invited to share a slice of its life. It includes a nameless stillness we've shared, a familiarity that lets us be silent together while other visitors tromp and chatter and toss rocks at its iceberg babies. It includes knowing that this glacier is more complex than I'll ever begin to comprehend. It includes feeling tenderness at the glacier's frailty in the face of warm sun. I've watched rocks plunk into the water as the glacial ice melts from beneath them.

As intensely as I love this glacier, as many tears as I shed, it can never be enough. Its beauty deserves so much more. Light is sluicing down the striped snowy slope behind it making the snowdrifts look like a crystal scarf that was solidified while waving in a gentle wind behind a magnificent being. Cavell Glacier is stunning.

You're so beautiful, I tell it. What else can I do?

A breeze comes up and chops the reflections on the pond into gold and turquoise flickers. I smile and shake my head. Words do not exist for this.

"There is not enough love to pour into you." I tell it. "Every moment you do something else beautiful. I love it. I love being overwhelmed and astonished and endlessly delighted by you. I also feel a little embarrassed at being so affected by you."

I wonder what it would be like to be part of a tribe who didn't think it was odd to passionately love nature, a tribe whose job, in fact, was to love nature? What if every night over dinner, family members asked me, "What did you love today? What did you touch? What touched you?"

My tribe and I would go together and love places. I would have been taught as a child not only to meditate or pray but also to love. My teachers would have said, "Love when you walk to the bus stop. Love when you see the grass between the cracks in the sidewalk. Love when you look up to the clouds or down to the dirt. Don't let an ice floe melt away without feeling well-loved first."

Yes, I wish that were my legitimate occupation and job description. I wish that could be the standard I'll be judged by when I die. The tribal elder and the angel at the gate to heaven will ask,

"Did you love nature well enough?"

Even if I were alone, the last of my tribe, I would like to be able to say, "I come from thousands of years of tradition, handed down in stories and rituals and training. My tribe's job is to love nature. My personal job is to love nature. I know there is value in my loving. Love rides and strengthens the cosmic superstrings that connect me and this mountain and this glacier and this tiny tree. I'm not just connected to them by the air they breathe to me and the air I breathe back. I'm connected to them by love.

I think about indigenous people in South America and Tibet and Mexico and the United States who feel their job is to worship the sun, or sing the sun up, or keep the earth's energy in balance through rituals and respect. They may do many other things in their lives, but being in right relationship to the earth and fulfilling their responsibilities to the earth are primary.

I want to belong to a tribe that says, "Every day love the earth. Every day stroke it and admire it and tell it how beautiful it is. Go to nature for inspiration or peace or answers, but most important, go to love it. Don't just love it theoretically or intellectually. Love it personally. Love this rock and this miniature fir tree and this ice floe. Love it with aching and tears."

And so, I add this to my life goals: to love nature. Not to love nature as a sideline or an afterthought, but to love it as a primary job. To open the flood-gates of my heart and love. Not to whisper or feel ashamed or silly. This is my job and I can do it with all my heart. This is my gift and I can give it freely, copiously, extravagantly.

I stand and face Cavell Glacier. "Good-bye, beautiful beloved. You may not be here when I return. You are dying"

You are dying, too, it replies. A spike of fear and sadness jolts through me. It's right.

It continues, *That's why you have to love now. You may be gone. I may be gone. Only this moment counts. Love now.*

I touch the sign by the parking lot as I leave. It reads: Elevation 11,033 feet. Nurse Edith Cavell was arrested by Germans on 8/15/15 on a charge of assisting English, Belgian, and French soldiers across the frontier. Executed 2 A.M., Oct. 12. She was matron of Surgical Institute of Brussels when war broke out. Refused to leave her post when fall of city was imminent.

NOTES

Initial quote

p. vii Martha Freeman, ed., *Always, Rachel: The Letters of Rachel Carson and Dorothy Freeman, 1952-1964* (Boston: Beacon Press, 1995), 231.

Introduction

p. 2 James A. Michener, *The Source* (New York: Random House, 1965), 153.

p. 4 Carl Sherman, "Be Happier! The Totally Natural Way to Lift Your Spirits," *McCall's*, September 1994, 124-25.

p. 5 H. Iltis, "Can One Love a Plastic Tree?" *Bull. Ecol. Soc. Amer.* 1973 (54:5-7). Quoted in Stephen R. Kellert and Edward O. Wilson, eds., *The Biophilia Hypothesis* (Washington, D.C.: Island Press, 1993), 65.

p. 5 Alan Watts, *Psychotherapy East and West* (New York: Pantheon Books, 1961), 96.

p. 5 Al Gore, *Earth in the Balance: Ecology and the Human Spirit* (New York: Penguin Group, 1992), 366.

p. 7 Gary Paul Nabhan and Stephen Trimble, *The Geography of Childhood: Why Children Need Wild Places* (Boston: Beacon Press, 1994), xxiii–iv. The quote from the Boston girl comes from the introduction by Robert Coles.

Chapter 1: Communing with Nature

p. 9 Martin Buber, *I and Thou* (New York: Charles Scribner's Sons, 1970), 57-58.

p. 9   Deepak Chopra, *The Seven Spiritual Laws of Success: A Practical Guide to the Fulfillment of Your Dreams* (San Rafael, Calif.: Amber-Allen, 1994), 23.

p. 16 Thich Nhat Hanh, *Peace Is Every Step: The Path of Mindfulness in Everyday Life* (New York: Bantam, 1991), 14–15.

Chapter 2: Getting Ready

p. 23 Ralph Waldo Emerson, *Nature,* as quoted in *Nature Walking* (Boston: Beacon Press, 1991), 14.

p. 24 Henry David Thoreau, *Walking,* as quoted in *Nature Walking* (Boston: Beacon Press, 1991), 78. *Walking* was originally published in 1862.

p. 26 Setting a later time to worry about an issue comes from the field of cognitive therapy pioneered by Aaron Beck and Albert Ellis. The technique is specifically described in Martin E. P. Seligman, *Learned Optimism* (New York: Alred A. Knopf, 1991), 217–18.

p. 36 Rupert Ross, *Dancing with a Ghost: Exploring Indian Reality* (Markham, Ontario: Reed Books Canada, 1992), 40.

p. 38 Tim Ward, *What the Buddha Never Taught* (Toronto: Somerville House, 1990; Berkeley, Calif.: Celestial Arts, 1993), 42.

Chapter 3: Settling In

p. 41 Joseph Campbell with Bill Moyers, *The Power of Myth* (New York: Doubleday, 1988), 5.

p. 43 Larry Dossey, M.D., is quoted in Liz Lufkin, "Slow Down, You Move Too Fast: The Time-Sickness Cure," *Working Woman,* April 1990, 112.

p. 43 Franz Kafka is quoted in Deepak Chopra, *The Seven Spiritual Laws of Success: A Practical Guide to the Fulfillment of Your Dreams* (San Rafael, Calif.: Amber-Allen, 1994), 20.

p. 47 Roger Bannister is quoted in Julia Cameron, *The Artist's Way* (New York: The Putnam Publishing Group, 1992), 185.

p. 47 Jon Kabat-Zinn, *Wherever You Go There You Are: Mindfulness Meditation in Everyday Life* (New York: Hyperion, 1994), xiii.

p. 48 Thought-stopping comes from the field of cognitive therapy pioneered by Aaron Beck and Albert Ellis. The technique is described in Martin E.P. Seligman, *Learned Optimism* (New York: Alfred A. Knopf, 1990), 217–18.

p. 48 Stephen Levine, *A Gradual Awakening* (Garden City, New York: Anchor Books/Doubleday, 1979), 22.

p. 50 The Nature Conservancy is a national organization that preserves plant and animal species by buying habitat. Their phone number is (703) 841-5300.

p. 51 Jeffrey Gold, Ph.D., taught this 4-3-2-1 technique in a hypnotherapy consultation group in Seattle in 1991. He attributed the technique to Milton Erickson, M.D.

Chapter 4: Using Silence

p. 58 Rabbi Dov Baer is quoted in Lawrence LeShan, *How to Meditate: A Guide to Self-Discovery* (Boston: Little, Brown & Co., 1974), 75.

p. 59 The quote from Luther Burbank comes from Peter Tompkins and Christopher Bird, *The Secret Life of Plants* (New York: Harper and Row, 1973), 27–28. It is from a lecture Burbank gave to the American Pomological Society.

p. 62 Sogyal Rinpoche, *The Tibetan Book of Living and Dying* (New York: HarperCollins, 1992), 68-69. For more on using your breath to settle your mind or meditate, see Lawrence LeShan, *How to Meditate* (Boston: Little, Brown & Co., 1974), 79-82 and 86; and David Fontana, *The Meditator's Handbook: A Comprehensive Guide to Eastern & Western Meditation Techniques* (Rockport, Mass.: Element, 1992), 33-36.

p. 66 R. W. Sanford, "The Personal Nature of Wilderness," *Banff National Park Newsletter* (Summer 1991), 8.

p. 74 Clarissa Pinkola Estes, *Women Who Run with the Wolves: Myths and Stories of the Wild Woman Archetype* (New York: Ballantine Books, 1992), 287.

Chapter 5: Using Words

p. 81 Annie Dillard, *Pilgrim at Tinker Creek* (New York: Harper's Magazine Press, 1974), 30-31.

Chapter 6: Using Mantras

p. 90 LeShan's Telephone Book Method is described in Lawrence LeShan, *How to Meditate* (Boston: Little, Brown & Co., 1974), 92-93.

p. 90 Swami Ramananda is quoted in Hilary Sterne, "Feeling More Frazzled Than Festive?" *Self,* December, 1994, 154.

p. 90 Diane Ackerman, *A Natural History of the Senses* (New York: Random House, 1990), 205.

p. 94 Annie Dillard, *Pilgrim at Tinker Creek* (New York: Harper's Magazine Press, 1974), 34.

p. 96 ". . . faith the size of a mustard seed" paraphrases

Matthew 17:20 from *The Holy Bible* (Grand Rapids, Mich: The Zondervan Bible Publishers, 1983), 718.

p. 97 Annie Dillard, *Pilgrim at Tinker Creek* (New York: Harper's Magazine Press, 1974), 259.

p. 100 Lenore Friedman, *Meetings with Remarkable Women: Buddhist Teachers in America* (Boston: Shambhala, 1987), 42–43, 80.

p. 101 Justin F. Stone, *The Joys of Meditation* (Albuquerque, New Mex.: Far West Pub. Co., 1973), 34.

p. 103 Milton Trager, M.D., and Cathy Guadagno-Hammond, *Trager Mentastics: movement as a way to agelessness* (Barrytown, New York: Station Hill Press, 1987). Page 9 mentions the blending process, p. 10 calls mentastics meditation-in-motion, and p. 32 lists the basic questions.

Chapter 7: Getting Close

p. 111 Jon Kabat-Zinn, *Wherever You Go There You Are: Mindfulness Meditation in Everyday Life* (New York: Hyperion, 1994), 69.

p. 113 Antoine de Saint-Exupery, *The Little Prince* (Orlando, Fla: Harcourt Brace Jovanovich, 1943), 96–97.

p. 114 Walt Whitman is quoted in Lawrence LeShan, *How to Meditate* (Boston: Little, Brown & Co., 1974), 88.

p. 119 Julia Cameron, *The Artist's Way* (New York: The Putnam Publishing Group, 1992), 53.

p. 119 Alan W. Watts, *Psychotherapy East and West* (New York: Pantheon Books, 1961), 112 and 173.

Chapter 8: Using Role Models

p. 123 The ant, the grasshopper, and the crow are characters in *Aesop's Fables.* Annette Harrison, "The Grasshopper and the Ant," *Easy-to-Tell Stories for Young Children* (Jonesborough, Tenn.: National Storytelling Press, 1952), 51. Michael Hague, "The Crow and the Pitcher," *Aesop's Fables* (New York: Holt, 1985), 11.

p. 123 Job 12:7-8, *Gold Seal Bible* (Philadelphia: National Bible Press, 1943), 588.

p. 124 The quote from Dogen is from his main work entitled *Shobogenzo,* quoted in Allan G. Grapard, "Nature and Culture in Japan." In Michael Tobias, ed., *Deep Ecology* (San Diego: Avant Books, 1985), 248.

p. 132 The quote by Stuart Udall is from his book *The Quiet Crisis* (1963), and is quoted in George Sessions, "Ecological Consciousness and Paradigm Change." In Michael Tobias, ed., *Deep Ecology* (San Diego: Avant Books, 1985), 35.

Chapter 9: Being-It

p. 137 Albert Schweitzer, *Indian Thought and Its Development* (Gloucester, Mass.: Beacon Press, 1936), 35. Schweitzer is quoting the Kaivalya Upanishad.

p. 145 Gregory Bateson, "Language and Psychotherapy," *Psychiatry* (vol. 21), 96, 100. Quoted in Alan Watts, *Psychotherapy East and West* (New York: Pantheon Books, 1961), 124–25.

p. 148 Albert Einstein is quoted by the editors of Conari Press in *Random Acts of Kindness* (Berkeley: Conari Press, 1993), 45.

Chapter 10: Reaching for the Essence

p. 153 Ralph Waldo Emerson, *Nature,* as quoted in *Nature Walking* (Boston: Beacon Press, 1991), 3.

Chapter 11: Coming Home

p. 169 Steven S. McFadden, *Profiles in Wisdom: Native Elders Speak about the Earth* (Santa Fe, New Mex.: Bear & Co., 1991), 124.

p. 171 Thomas Berry, *The Dream of the Earth* (San Francisco: Sierra Club Books, 1988), 1–2.

p. 173 L. M. Wolfe, ed., *John Muir, John of the Mountains: The Unpublished Journals of John Muir,* quoted in Barbara K. Rodes and Rice Odell, *A Dictionary of Environmental Quotations* (New York: Simon & Schuster, 1992).

ABOUT THE AUTHOR

Ruth Baetz, MSW, began her relationship with nature in the backyards and alleys of Chicago. Now she communes in the green spaces near her home in Seattle, Washington; on the slopes of her touchstone, Mount Rainier; and everywhere she travels. She has volunteered with The Nature Conservancy and the Conservation Division of the Mountaineers.

Ruth received her Master's of Social Work from the University of Washington. She has worked at Family Services of King County and has been a therapist in private practice for over fifteen years, counseling women who are recovering from trauma or who are going through life transitions and psychological growth spurts. She has given trainings at universities, agencies, and conferences, and has spoken on radio and television shows.

A ghostwriter, writer, and editor, Ruth is the co-author of *We Did the Best We Could* and the author of *Lesbian Crossroads*.

Hazelden Publishing and Education is a division of the Hazelden Foundation, a not-for-profit organization. Since 1949, Hazelden has been a leader in promoting the dignity and treatment of people afflicted with the disease of chemical dependency.

The mission of the foundation is to improve the quality of life for individuals, families, and communities by providing a national continuum of information, education, and recovery services that are widely accessible; to advance the field through research and training; and to improve our quality and effectiveness through continuous improvement and innovation.

Stemming from that, the mission of the publishing division is to provide quality information and support to people wherever they may be in their personal journey—from education and early intervention, through treatment and recovery, to personal and spiritual growth.

Although our treatment programs do not necessarily use everything Hazelden publishes, our bibliotherapeutic materials support our mission and the Twelve Step philosophy upon which it is based. We encourage your comments and feedback.

The headquarters of the Hazelden Foundation are in Center City, Minnesota. Additional treatment facilities are located in Chicago, Illinois; New York, New York; Plymouth, Minnesota; St. Paul, Minnesota; and West Palm Beach, Florida. At these sites, we provide a continuum of care for men and women of all ages. Our Plymouth facility is designed specifically for youth and families.

For more information on Hazelden, please call 1-800-257-7800. Or you may access our World Wide Web site on the Internet at http://www.hazelden.org.